THE WISDOM
OF THE PROPHETS
(Fusus al-Hikam)

MUHYI-D-DIN IBN 'ARABI

THE WISDOM
OF THE PROPHETS
(Fusus al-Hikam)

Translated from Arabic to French
with notes by
TITUS BURCKHARDT

Translated from French to English by
ANGELA CULME-SEYMOUR

BESHARA PUBLICATIONS

© Beshara Design Centre 1975

Published by Beshara Publications
Swyre Farm, Aldsworth
Gloucestershire

ISBN 0 904975 00 2

Printed by The Compton Press Ltd.
Compton Chamberlayne, Salisbury
Wiltshire

Contents

Translator's Introduction

As soon as I read Titus Burckhardt's excellent French text of the Fusus al-Hikam I determined to find out whether there existed an English translation. Evidently there was none; and the idea came to me that I must attempt to translate it from the French myself.

After the first few readings I found the Fusus comparable to a large and detailed canvas: the more often I read it the more I understood; meanings that had at first seemed ambiguous suddenly became clear; certain lines read for the third time were as moving as the first time, and always there was – and still is – something new and of a profound interest to be discovered – or rather realized, by which I mean grasped with a sudden intuitive understanding, as well as intellectually.

Titus Burckhardt, in his introduction, dwells mostly on Ibn 'Arabi's philosophy and terminology, an essential overture to the understanding of this unique book; but he says little of Ibn 'Arabi's life.

Muhyi-d-din Ibn 'Arabi was born, as we know, at Murcia in Spain in the year 1165, but the day of his birth is uncertain. It was probably August 7th – though some sources say July 28th – at any rate it was the 27th day of Ramadan, significantly, the Night of Power, the Night of which is written in the Koran: '. . . the night of Kadr is better than a thousand months, therein do the angels descend, the Spirit also, by the permission of their Lord, with his decrees concerning every matter. It is peace until the breaking of dawn'.

Ibn 'Arabi came from an ancient Arab family and his parents had many Sufis and mystics among their friends. He was brought up, there-fore, in an atmosphere conducive to the following of the Sufi Way. He started seriously to study when he and his family fled to Seville in 1173 after the Almohads occupied Murcia.

Even at an early age his innate spiritual understanding, his aptitude to meditation, prayer, fasting, and other practices of the Sufi Way, as well as his ability to study the metaphysical doctrines and other sciences of Sufi inclination, both astonished and commanded the respect of his teachers, many of whom even allowed him to pass on their own teachings.

In the year 1184 it is thought that he met in Cordova for the first time his father's friend Averroes – Ibn Rushd – a well known philosopher and mystic, and in the same year he embarked on the Sufi Way.

From then on he continued to study, to teach, to write, and later, to travel; he also married his 'saintly wife' called Maryam, of whom no more is known. He was later to marry at least three times more, a Konya woman as recounted below; Fatimah, daughter of a Sharif of Mecca; and lastly a daughter of the Chief Qadi of Damascus.

He had numerous teachers and met countless Sufis and other holy men and saints, two of whom particularly impressed him, both being women : Shams of Marchena and Fatimah of Cordova. Many of them are described in his two books translated under the title of *Sufis of Andalusia* by R. W. Y. Austin (George Allen & Unwin), who also gives a short but comprehensive account of his life.

There is no room here to give details of his extensive travels; he was thirty years of age when he started and he went to Fez, Marrakesh, Tunis, Cairo, Alexandria, Mecca, Baghdad, and Aleppo; to Kayseri, Malatya and Konya where there still exist (as in Istanbul and Baghdad) some manuscripts in his own hand, and where he married the mother of Sadr ud Din-i-Qunawi, one of his closest disciples, to whom he left many of his works. Here also a link was formed, which was of enormous importance, between him and the great Persian poet and mystic Jalálu'ddín Rúmí, founder of the Mevlevi order of Dervishes. He went also to Medina, Jerusalem and Damascus as well as Granada, Rota, Tarifa and many other towns in Spain. It was in Fez that many of the dramatic incidents of his life took place : he met the Pole of the time there, he gathered a large number of students and disciples, and in the year 1199 he learnt of the Seal of Muhammedan Sainthood, revealing his own spiritual state. That he himself was the Seal of Muhammedan Sainthood was revealed to him later, in Mecca.

Nor is there room nor necessity – since they are to be found in *Sufis of Andalusia* – to describe here his varied and extraordinary relationships with the other great mystics and Sufis, his remarkable revelations and visions, and manifestations, his three meetings with Khidr, the attempts on his life, nor even his audiences with the kings and rulers of the time, like Kay Kaus of Anatolia or King al-Malik al-Zahir, King of Antioch, over whom he had considerable influence.

With all his travelling he wrote over three hundred – probably more – books, many of which are now lost, and most of which, he says, were written not through study and his own composition but by revelations from God. Indeed, at the close of the chapter on Adam in the Fusus he says: '. . . I have transcribed in this book that portion which was assigned to me, and not everything which I have realized; for that no book in the present world could contain . . . '. The Fusus, one of the shortest, was however, regarded by him as one of the most important : the nucleus, as it were, of his teaching and philosophy. He was probably the first great mystic to put into writing what had hitherto only been learnt by word of mouth.

Before he died in Damascus on November 16th, 1240 at the age of 76, leaving two sons and a daughter, his spiritual state had reached a very high order. He was famous, and regarded with veneration and awe. Recognized as one of the greatest mystics, if not the greatest mystic of all time, he was, in fact, known among Sufis as Al-Shaikh al Akbar – the greatest Shaikh.

The influence of Muhyi-d-din Ibn 'Arabi was and is immense. This, in addition to the beauty, the knowledge imparted, and the unique quality of his writings are the reasons why I feel, with the growing interest in the west in mysticism and Sufi doctrines, that his work should be more widely and easily available in English.

I am grateful to Bulent Rauf, for his help, and for first introducing me to the Fusus; to Grenville Collins for his help in research; to Drusilla for typing the first copy; and to Hugh Tollemache and Simon Blackwood for their help in making this publication possible.

Bitez 1975   ANGELA CULME SEYMOUR

Introduction

(from the translation into French by Titus Burckhardt)

THE Sufi Abu Bakr Muhammed ibn al-Arabi[1] of the Arabic tribe of Hâtim at-Tâ'î was born in the year 560 of the Hegira (the year 1165 of the Christian era) at Murcia in Andalusia; he died in 638 (A.D. 1240) in Damascus. In esoteric circles of Islam he is called *muhyi-d-dîn*, 'the animator of religion', and '*ash-sheikh al-akbar*', 'the greatest master'. His doctrinal work imposes itself by its depths and by its synthesis, as well as by the incisive form of certain formulations, which refer to the most elevated aspects of Sufism. The books and treatises of the master were very numerous; most of them seem to be definitely lost; amongst those that survive the *Futûhât al-Makkiyah* ('The revelations of Mecca') and the *Fusûs al-Hikam* ('The Wisdom of the Prophets') are the most celebrated. The former of these two works constitutes a sort of sum of esoteric sciences; the latter, of which we present here a translation limited to the most important chapters, is often considered as the spiritual testament of the master, who drafted it in the year 627 of the Hegira (A.D. 1229) in Damascus.

We must specify that the title 'Wisdom of the Prophets' is only a paraphrase, henceforth consecrated by the use of the Arab title of *Fusûs al-Hikam,* which signifies literally 'the settings of the Wisdom'. This expression does not so much define the contents of the book but summarizes it symbolically, and could not be understood without the preliminary knowledge of the symbolism in question : *al-fass* – singular of *fusûs* – is the setting which holds the stone or the seal (*al-khatam*) of a ring; by 'the Wisdom' (*al-hikam*), one must understand here the aspects of the Divine Wisdom. The 'settings' which hold the precious stones of the eternal Wisdom (*al-hikmah*) are the spiritual 'forms' of

[1] The spelling Ibn al 'Arabi is more correct; however one currently employs the form Ibn 'Arabi, so as to distinguish it from the celebrated Sufi, the Andalusian Abu Bakr ibn al-'Arabi.

[1]

different Prophets, their respective natures, both human and spiritual, which transport such or such an aspect of the Divine Knowledge. The incorruptible character of the precious stone corresponds to the unchanging nature of Wisdom.

The metaphor of the setting which encloses the precious stone of the Wisdom, and encircles its form, concerns the human nature of a prophet in so far as he is the recipient of the Divine Wisdom; however, this aspect of symbolism, which corresponds to the human appearance of things, is to be found compensated and as if enlarged by the formula that Ibn 'Arabi adopts for the titles of the various parts of his book: 'The setting of the Divine Wisdom in the Word of Adam', 'The setting of the Wisdom of the Divine Inspiration in the Word of Seth', 'The setting of the Wisdom of the Transcendence in the Word of Noah' etc. According to these expressions, the setting, that is to say the individual form of the prophet, is in its turn contained in the Word (al-kalimah), which is the essential and Divine reality of this same prophet; in fact by its 'active' identification with the Divine Wisdom, each prophet is an immediate determination of the eternal Word, which is the primordial 'enunciation' of God. It is the 'words' which contain the 'settings', for it is the individual who is contained by the universal and not inversely, in spite of human appearances. Every prophet, as Perfect Man, 'contains', then, himself, since he 'contains' the Divine Wisdom, and, in relation to his interior and 'supra-individual' reality he 'is' this Wisdom; now, this latter contains the perfect humanity of the Man-God, and it is this aspect of things which corresponds to the ontological reality, without annulling, however, the 'reality' which is apparent from the human point of view. Finally, we must not forget to add that the humanity of the prophets, which, by definition, is perfect and 'without equal', reflects in its particularity – the 'setting' (fass) which has such or such a form – or such an aspect of a Divine Name, which comes back to saying that the prophet identifies himself in the final analysis to this Name, this latter 'opening the way' to the Divine Indifferentiated Essence.

This apparently contradictory complexity of aspects, integrated in a suprarational synthesis, is characteristic in the teaching of Ibn 'Arabi.

The connection between the 'setting' and the Wisdom which it contains, and which is in its turn the content, prefigures the fundamental theme of the Fusûs al-Hikam, a theme which can be summarized in the following manner: the Divine revelation complies with the recep-

[2]

tivity of the heart, the same as light, without the colour in itself, is coloured according to the crystal which refracts it; the aspect that the Divinity assumes then, depends on its 'recipient'. On the other hand the Divine Reality being active and creating, whereas the 'recipient' is passive, all positive qualities by which God manifests Himself, must emanate from Him; these are the real contents of the Divine Essence which determine the quality of a contemplative state. Finally, according to a point of view even more vast, the receptacle, that is to say the heart of man, or more exactly his essential and integral being, is itself a divine possibility; it is this permanent and informal possibility, the archetype, which the most immediately receives the Divine Light.

The divine Reality, then, englobes at once the recipient of the revelation and its contents; one knows it only by the law itself of its manifestation, so that one distinguishes it from its receptacles without however separating, essentially and in all aspects, the receptacles and the Reality.

Man, who is the receptacle 'par excellence' of the Divine revelation, must, in order to know God, know himself, in his permanent possibility. But, he will know himself, only through God; in so far as He is himself the object of the knowledge, God is the 'subject', the transcendent Witness; in so far as God is the 'object' of the knowledge, He colours Himself according to the subject who contemplates Him.

If there is, in the doctrinal teaching of Ibn 'Arabi, some sort of system, it is the permutation of opposing and complementary terms. This methodical employ of paradox allows no truce to the spirit of the reader, naturally inclined to 'fix' himself on a definite, 'dogmatic' notion if you like, and it pushes him towards that which Ibn 'Arabi himself calls *'al-hayrah'*, that is to say 'perplexity' or 'astonishment' before that which surpasses rational order; this *hayrah,* he says, must become a constant circular movement round a point mentally incomprehensible, an image which recalls the last verses of the Divine Comedy : '. . . Such was I at the time of this new vision; I wanted to see how much the (human) image fitted to the (divine) circle, and how it integrated itself. But for that my own wings do not suffice. My spirit was struck by a flash, and at once my will was accomplished. Here at the highest spiritual degree of imagination, the forces were failing; but already my desire and my will were turning, like a wheel which is uniformly put in motion by the Love which moves the sun and other stars'.

Certain statements of Ibn 'Arabi may appear incoherent not only for the reason which we have just indicated, but also because intellectual inspiration, evoking at once innumerable truths which are jointly and separately liable, exerts a sort of pressure on the too narrow recipient, which is discursive thought, and tends to break the 'horizontal' continuity; for an analogous reason, the epistles of St. Paul may seem incoherent. The intrinsic plenitude of the contemplative perception, without common measure of reason, will produce formulas supersaturated with meanings, whereas it prevents in a certain manner the homogeneous and definite construction of a system, which in any case would be too limited to 'exhaust' an aspect of the divine Truth. The more the statements of Ibn 'Arabi are essential, the more they are discontinuous; the completely nomad character of the Arab spirit, its power more plastic than incisive, seems there to be turned to profit by inspiration.

We will not return here to the terminology of which the master makes use, for we have talked of it in our study of Sufism[2] which one can consider in this respect as an introduction on to the *Fusûs al-Hikam*. We may also refer to our partial translation of *al-Insân al-kâmil* of Jîlî[3] which is presented as an exposé, more constructive, and more explicit, of certain fundamental ideas contained in the *Fusûs al-Hikam*. There is moreover, between the language of Ibn 'Arabi and Jîlî, the mental gap between the XII and the XIV centuries; that which the former expresses implicitly, the latter makes precise in a manner more articulate, at the price of a certain delimitation of realities.

As we have just seen, each chapter of the *Fusûs al-Hikam* is dedicated to a prophet, that is to say one of the prophets mentioned in the Koran, starting with Adam – considered in Islam as a prophet – until Muhammed who 'seals' the universal 'prophethood'. The Koranic chain of prophets includes also Christ and certain prophets of the ancient people of Arabia, like Salîh and Hûd, which the Judo-Christian writings do not know. The base and point of departure of each chapter is a passage of writing, the most often a word of the Koran attributed to one of the prophets.

---

[2] *Introduction aux doctrines esoteriques de L'Islam,* (P. Derain, Lyon et Messerschmitt, Alger 1955); and, *An Introduction to Sufi Doctrine,* (Sh. Mohammed Ashraf, Lahore).

[3] De l'homme universal Ibid, 1953.

Amongst the 27 chapters of the work, we have chosen those which, by their doctrinal content seem to us the most important. We have omitted the chapters or the parts of the chapters of which the content is more particular, or which contain exegesis too difficult to render into a European language; for the Sufi interpretation of the Koran is often founded on a verbal symbolism belonging to the Arabic language. In a certain sense the first two chapters, on Adam and on Seth, summarize in themselves the metaphysical doctrine of Ibn 'Arabi in the double relationship of the universal manifestation of God and of the spiritual realization.

Amongst the books which have been written on Muhyi-d-dîn Ibn 'Arabi in European languages, the most important, and even the only work of merit, is *El Islam Christianizado* by Miguel Asin Palacios.[4] This work passes in silence over the metaphysics of Ibn 'Arabi, but on the other hand it describes his life and his spiritual method, of which he gives some most precious glimpses, in spite of the general tendance, which is announced in the title itself of the book and which is at the base of abusive assimilations; struck by the saintliness of certain Sufis, Palacios wishes to justify them before the Christian dogma, considering them as representatives of a Christian tendency in the framework of Islam. To this end he makes them derive their method of monastic traditions from Oriental Christianity. But, if, certainly, there have been contacts between the first Sufis and the Christian contemplatives – certain Islamic witnesses confirm it, – the most part of the analogies that Palacios invokes in favour of his thesis are those which are to be found in the most diverse civilizations. As for the fundamental role which the Koran plays in Sufism, Palacios is of the opinion that the 'Judeo-Christian elements' contained in the Koran compensate for the lack of authenticity, as if the truth could be transported by a lie or as if a spiritual way was not an organic total, wherein everything is to be found, so that the smallest element may have incalculable consequences. However it may be, the work in question gives an aspect on the spirituality of Ibn 'Arabi which a purely metaphysical work like the *Fusûs al-Hikam* could make one lose sight of; we must insist then, in stressing that our book will be unable to give a complete idea of the way of our Sufi. Ibn 'Arabi observes himself that the perfection of the spiritual virtues may provoke the illumination of the heart, even without the man having a theoretical knowledge going beyond the elemen-

[4] Madrid 1931, Ed. Plutarco.

tary truths of the doctrine, whereas the comprehension of the meta-physical theory does not guarantee his effective realization. Let us add that there have been Sufis who taught only the 'polishing of the mirror of the heart' and remained silent on the transcendent Truths (al haqâiq), rather like certain Buddhist masters limited themselves to teaching the rejection of psychological limitations.

M. Asin Palacios has also published a Spanish translation of Risâlat al-Quds ('The Epistle of Sanctity') of Ibn 'Arabi, under the title of Vidas de Santones Andaluces;[5] this book describes the lives of Sufis that Ibn 'Arabi knew in Spain and who were for the most part his own spiritual masters.

It is not surprising – in view of the obscurity of our author – that the number of his writings translated into European languages be so restricted. Let us mention the English translation – by Reynold A. Nicholson – of Tarjumân al-ashwâq ('The interpreter of Desires') a collection of poems of love with esoteric commentaries.[6] An excellent translation of 'Treatise on Unity' (Risâlat al-Ahadiyah), attributed to Muhyi-d-dîn Ibn 'Arabi, has been published by Abdul Hadi in the review La Voile d'Isis.[7] The Arabic text of three minor treatises of Ibn 'Arabi, under the title of Kleinere Schriften des Ibn al-'Arabi has been edited by Nyberg, who has given a resumé of it in German.[8] As for the book of Khaja Khan : The Wisdom of the Prophets,[9] it represents only a free paraphrase of the Fusûs al-Hikam.

For our translation we have used the edition lithographed in Cairo, in the year of 1309 of the Hegira (A.D. 1891) made by Muhammed al-Bârûnî, with the commentary by 'Abd ar Razzâq al-Qashânî and the typographic edition of 1304 (1887), made by Jalâl ad-dîn Uskûbî, with commentaries by 'Abd al-Ghanî an-Nâbulusî and by 'Abd ar-Rahmân al-Jâmî. These three commentators are well known Sufis; an-Nâbulusî lived at the end of the XII and beginning of the XIII century, al Qashânî in the XIII and al-Jâmî in the XV century of the Christian era. We have not considered it useful to translate these commentaries, for the exigencies of the European reader with regard

[5] Publicaciones de las Escuelas de estudios arabes de Madrid y Granada, serie B.
[6] In Oriental Translation Fund of the Royal Asiatic Society, new series Vol. XX. H.S.
[7] Paris, February 1933.
[8] Leiden, 1919. Ed. E. J. Brill.
[9] Madras, 1929.

to a commentary differ a great deal to those of the oriental reader; on the other hand, we have completed the translation by some notes and sometimes interpolations – given in brackets – where it has seemed to us indispensable; all modern translation from an Arabic text written in an elliptical language of the XII century necessitates a certain amount of exigent work.

Of the Divine Wisdom
(al-hikmat al-ilâhiyah)
in the Word of Adam

GOD *(al-haqq)* wanted to see the essences *(al-a'yan)*[1] of His most perfect Names *(al-asmâ al-husnâ)* whose number is infinite – and if you like you can equally well say : God wanted to see His own Essence *('ayn)*[2] in one global object *(kawn)* which having been blessed with existence *(al-wujûd)*[3] summarized the Divine Order *(al-amr)*[4] so that there He could manifest His mystery *(sirr)* to Himself.[5]

For the vision *(ru'yâ)*[6] that a being[7] has of himself in himself is not the same as that which another reality procures for him, and which

[1] *A'yân* is translated here as 'essences', since it concerns the essences of the Names as opposed to their verbal or thought forms. The object of the divine 'vision' resides in the essential possibilities which correspond to the 'Most Perfect Names', meaning the universal and permanent 'aspects' of the Being. When one speaks of the *one* and single Essence of all the Divine Names and Qualities, one employs the term *adh-dhât*.

[2] The word *al-'ayn* (singular of *a'yân*) contains the meanings of 'essential determination', 'personal essence', 'archetype', 'eye', 'source'. This sentence signifies then, that God wanted to see Himself, with the restriction that His 'vision' does not refer to His Absolute Essence *(adh-dhât)*, which transcends all determination, even principial, but to His immediate determination *('aynah)*, His 'personal aspect', which is precisely characterized by the Perfect Qualities of which the Names are the expression.

[3] Or of the Being, the term *al-wujûd* having the two meanings. Some manuscripts give the variant: '. . . being endowed with faces *(al-wujûh)* . . .' that is to say with multiple 'planes of reflection' differentiating the Divine irradiation *(at-tajallî)*.

[4] The Divine Order is symbolized by the word 'be!' *(kun)*; it identifies itself then, to the principle of existence.

[5] The allusion to the Divine Word *(hadîth qudsî)* revealed by the mouth of the Prophet: 'I was a hidden treasure; I loved to be known (or: know) and I created the world'.

[6] The visual act is here taken as the symbol of Knowledge in its universal nature.

[7] Literally: 'the thing' *(ash-shay)*. Ibn Arabi sometimes employs the term 'thing' to designate a reality which he does not want to define in any way; he

[8]

he uses for himself as a mirror : in this he manifests himself to his self in the form which results from the 'place' of the vision; this would not exist without the 'plane of reflection' and the ray which is reflected therein.

God first created the entire world as something amorphous[8] and without grace[9] comparable to a mirror not yet polished;[10] but it is a rule in the Divine activity to prepare no 'place' without it receiving a Divine spirit as is explained (in the Koran) by the blowing of the Divine spirit into Adam;[11] and this is none other (from a complementary point of view to the former), than the actualization of the aptitude (*al-isti'dâd*) which such a form possesses, having already the predisposition for it, to receive the inexhaustible effusion (*al-fayd*)[12] of the essential revelation (*at-tajallî*).[13]

There is not then (apart from the Divine Reality) other than one pure receptacle (*qâbil*);[14] but this receptacle itself comes from the Holy

---

does not say 'the Essence' (*adh-dhat*), so as not to affirm to the transcendance and the non-manifestation of that which is in question, and neither does he say the 'Being' or 'the Existence' (*al-wujûd*), so as not to emphasize thereby the immanence and the manifestation.

[8] Or 'homogeneous' (*musawwi*), that is to say not yet including the qualitative and differentiated imprint of the spirit.

[9] *Rawh* : 'grace', liberty; some read *rûh*, 'spirit'.

[10] It is the primordial chaos, where the possibilities of manifestation, still virtual, are lost in the indifferentiation of their *materia*.

[11] 'When I shall have formed him, and I shall have breathed my spirit into him' (Koran XV, 29).

[12] The image of an 'effusion', of an 'overflowing' or of an 'emanation' of the Being (*al-wujûd*) or of the divine Light (*an-nûr*) in the receptive 'forms' of the world must not be understood as a substantial emanation, for the Being – or the increated divine Light – does not proceed outside of Himself. This image expresses on the contrary the sovereign superabundance of the divine Reality, which deploys and illuminates the relative possibilities of the world, although It be 'rich in Itself' (*ghanî binafsih*) and the existence of the world adds nothing to His infinity. – The symbolism of the divine 'effusion' (*al-fayd*) refers to this word of the Prophet: 'God has created the world in darkness, and then He poured (*afâda*) on it of His light'.

[13] *At-tajallî* signifies 'revelation' in a general sense) 'unveiling' and 'irradiation': when the sun, covered by clouds is 'unveiled', its light 'irradiates' over the earth.

[14] From the cosmological point of view, this receptacle corresponds to the passive substance, the 'materia prima' or the plastic principle of a world or of a being. From a purely metaphysical point of view, the receptacle which opposes – in a manner entirely principial and logical – the incessant 'effusion' of the Being, is reduced to the principial possibility, the archetype or the 'immutable essence' (*al-ayn ath-thâbitah*) of a world or a being.

Effusion (*al-fayd al-aqdas*) (that is to say from the principial manifestation, meta-cosmic, where the 'immutable Essences' are Divinely 'conceived' before their apparent projection in the relative existence).[15] For,
the entire reality (*al-amr*)[16] from its beginning to its end comes from
God alone, and it is to Him that it returns.[17] So, then, the Divine Order
required the clarification of the mirror of the world; and Adam
became the light itself of this mirror and the spirit of this form.[18]

As for the Angels (of whom there is some mention in the Koran's
account of Adam's creation),[19] they represent certain faculties of this

---

[15] This passage is explained as follows by the Persian Sufi Nur ad-dîn 'Abd
Rahmân Jâmî: 'The Majesty of God (*al-haqq*) reveals itself in two ways; one
of them, which corresponds to the interior revelation, purely intelligible, which
the Sufis call the most-saintly Effusion (*al-fayd al-aqdas*), consists in the self-
revelation of God manifesting Himself from all eternity to Himself in the form
of archetypes and that which they imply of characters and capacities; the second
revelation, is the exterior manifestation, objective, which is called saintly Effusion
(*al-fayd al-muqaddas*); it consists in the manifestation of God by means of the
imprint of the same archetypes. This second revelation is consecutive to the first;
it is the theatre where the perfections appear, which, according to the first
revelation, are virtually contained in the characters and the capacities of the
archetypes'. (*Lawaih,* ch. XXX; Persian text edition and English translation by
E. H. Whinfield and Mirza Muhammed Kazvini: Oriental translation Fund,
New series, Vol XVI Royal Asiatic Society). In this text the expressions 'forms'
or 'characters', which refer to the archetypes, should be understood as simple
'allusions', for the archetypes or 'immutable essences' are evidently beyond all
individualization or formal distinction.

[16] The word *amr* signifies primarily 'order', 'commandment', but contains also
the sense of 'reality' and of 'act'. The Divine Order 'be!' corresponds to the pure
Act.

[17] 'His is the kingdom of heaven and earth; and unto God shall all realities
return' (*al umûr,* that is to say increated realities of creatures) (Koran LVII, 5).

[18] In the original text, all the first part of the chapter, until the above words,
form one sentence, with several incidental propositions; it is a logical whole
describing all the essential aspects of the Divine Manifestation.

[19] 'When thy Lord said unto the angels: Verily, I am going to place a repre-
sentative on earth, they said: Wilt thou place there one who will sow corruption
therein, and shed blood?, whereas we celebrate Thy praise, and sanctify Thee.
He answered: Verily I know that which ye know not; and he taught Adam the
Names of all things, and then showed them to the angels, and said: Declare unto
Me the Names of these things if you say the truth. They answered, Praise unto
Thee, we have no knowledge, but what Thou teachest us, for Thou art Knowing
and Wise! He said: O Adam, let them know their names! And when he had
let them know their names, He said: Did I not tell you that I know the secrets
of heaven and earth, and I know that which you discover and that which you
conceal? And when We said unto the Angels prostrate yourselves before Adam,
they all prostrated themselves except Iblis (the devil) who refused, and was
puffed up with pride, and became of the number of unbelievers'. (Koran II, 28).

'form'[20] of the world which the Sufis call the Great Man (al-insân al-kabîr) so that the angels are to it just as the spiritual and physical faculties are to the human organism.[21] Each of these (cosmic) faculties finds itself as if veiled by its own nature; it conceives nothing which is superior to its own (relative) essence; for there is in it something which considers itself to be worthy of high rank and in the state nearest to God. It is thus because it participates (in a certain manner) in the Divine Synthesis (al-jam-'iyat al-ilâhiyah)[22] which governs that which appertains, be it to the Divine side (al-janâb al-ilâhî),[23] be it to the side of the Reality of Realities (haqîqat al-haqâïq),[24] be it again – and by this organism, support of all the faculties, – to the Universal Nature (tabî'at al-kull)[25]; this encompasses all the receptacles (qawabil) of the world, from its peak to its foundation.[26] But this, logical reasoning will not understand, for this sort of knowledge is solely dependent on Divine intuition (al-kashf al-ilâhî); it is by that alone that one will know the

[20] The expression 'form' (sûrah) is one of those which the Sufi authors use in a very free way, for it is susceptible of various transpositions beyond the closest significance, that of 'delimitation'; the form of a thing contains a purely qualitative aspect, the quality being of essential nature; on the other hand, in so far as the form of a being is opposed to its spirit, it symbolically returns to the receptive function of the materia.

[21] According to the Sufi adage: 'Man is a little cosmos, and the cosmos is like a big man'.

[22] Divine Uniqueness by virtue of which every being is unique.

[23] The 'Divine Side' is the sum of the Divine Qualities, the Divinity in so far as It produces and dominates the world, (the 'creature side').

[24] The 'Reality of Realities' or 'Truth of Truths' corresponds to the Word (Logos) as 'place' of all the possibilities of manifestation. It is the eternal mediator, the 'Reality of Muhammed' (al-haqîqat al-muhammadiyah), the 'Isthmus' (barzakh) between the pure Being and relative existence, the same as between the non-manifestation and the manifestation. It is the prototype of everything; there is nothing which does not bear its imprint.

[25] Universal Nature is the universal receptive power, the 'matrix' of the cosmos. According to the Hellenistic cosmologists, Nature is reduced to the plastic principle of the formal world, to the root of the four elements and of the four sensible qualities which rule all the changes of the physical order. Ibn Arabi, transposing the elements in the total cosmic order, attributes to Nature a far vaster function, co-extensive with all manifestation, including the angelic states. It is thus analogous to that which the Hindus designate as Mâyâ or as the universal Shakti, maternal and dynamic aspect of Prakpiti, the Substance or 'Materia Prima'. Let us add nevertheless that this principle does not play, in the teaching of Ibn 'Arabi, the same fundamental role that it assumes in the Advaïtic doctrine, since Islam considers the productive functions of the universe in an eminently 'theocentric' manner.

[26] The creature 'claims' then, to the totality by virtue at once of his Divine origin, of his universal prototype, and of his natural root.

roots of the forms of the world, in so far as they are receptive towards their ruling spirit.[27]

Thus, this being (Adamic) was called Man (*insân*) and God's Representative (*khalîfah*). As for his quality as a man it designates his synthesised nature (containing virtually all other natures created) and his aptitude to embrace the essential Truths. Man is to God (*al-haqq*) that which the pupil is to the eye (the pupil in Arabic is called 'man within the eye'), the pupil being that by which seeing is effected; for through him (that is to say the Universal Man) God contemplates His creation and dispenses His mercy. Thus is man at once ephemeral and eternal, a being created perpetual and immortal, a Verb discriminating (by his distinctive knowledge) and unifying (by his divine essence).[28] By his existence the world was completed. He is to the world that which the setting is to the ring; the setting carries the seal which the King applies to his treasure chests; and it is for this that (Universal) Man is called the Representative of God, Whose creation he safeguards, as one safeguards the treasures by a seal; as long as the King's seal is to be found on the treasure chests, nobody dares open them without his permission; thus man finds himself entrusted with the Divine safe-keeping of the world, and the world will not cease to be safeguarded as long as this Universal Man (*al-insân al-kâmil*) lives in it. Dost thou not see, then, that when he disappears and is taken away from the treasure chests of this lower world, nothing of which God kept in them will remain and all that they contained will go, each part joining its own (corresponding) part; everything will be transported into the other world, and (Universal Man) will be the seal on the coffers in the other world perpetually.

All that the Divine Form implies, that is to say the total of the names (or Universal Qualities) is manifested in this human constitution, which, by this means, distinguishes itself (from all other creatures) by the (symbolic) integration of all existence. From there comes the Divine argument condemning the Angels (who did not see the 'raison d'etre' nor the intrinsic superiority of Adam); remember that, for God exhorts thee by the example of others and see from whence the

[27] 'Abd ar-Razzâq al Qashânî specifies that reason, which is itself engendered by the polarity of the active and passive, of the Divine Order (*al-amr*) and of Nature (*at-tabî'ah*) cannot exceed this polarity and comprehend it 'from above'.

[28] These are the two aspects of all revealed words, to which refer the two designations of the Koran as 'Recitation' (*al-qu'rân*) and as 'Discrimination' (*al-furqân*).

judgement strikes that whom it strikes. The Angels did not realize what is implied by the constitution of this representative (of God on earth), and neither did they realize what is implied by the essential adoration (*dhâtiyah*) of God; for each does not know of God except that which he infers from himself. But, the Angels do not have the integral nature of Adam; so they did not comprehend the Divine Names, the knowledge of which is the privilege of this nature and by which this 'praises' Him (affirming His aspects of Beauty and Goodness) and 'proclaims' Him 'Holy' (attesting His essential Transcendence); they did not know that God possesses Names that were withdrawn from their knowledge and by which therefore they could not 'praise' Him nor 'proclaim' Him 'Holy'.

They were victims of their own limitations when they said, with regard to the creation (of Adam on earth); 'Wouldst Thou, then, create therein a being that sows corruption?'. Now, this corruption, what is it if not precisely the revolt that they themselves were manifesting? That which they were saying about Adam applies to their own attitude towards God. Moreover, if such a possibility (of revolt) was not in their nature, they would not have unconsciously affirmed it with regard to Adam; if they had had the knowledge of themselves they would have been exempt, by this very knowledge, from the limits to which they were submitted; they would not have insisted (in their accusation of Adam) so far as to draw vanity from their own 'praise' of God and from that by which they 'proclaimed' Him 'Holy', whereas Adam realised Names of which the Angels were ignorant, so that neither their 'praise' (*tasbîh*) nor their 'proclamation of Divine Holiness' (*taqdîs*) were the same as those of Adam.

This, God describes to us so that we should be on our guard, and that we should learn the right attitude towards Him – may He be exalted! – free from pretentiousness on matters which we have realised or embraced by our individual knowledge; moreover, how could we think we possess something which surpasses us (in its universal reality) and which we do not really know (essentially)? So pay attention to this Divine instruction on the way God punishes the most obedient and faithful of His servants, His closest representatives (according to the general hierarchy of beings).

But let us return now to the (Divine) Wisdom (in Adam). We can say of it that the Universal Ideas (*al-umur al-kulliyah*),[29] which

---

[29] The 'universals' according to scholastic terminology.

evidently have no individual existence as such, are none the less present, intelligibly and distinctly, in the mental state; they always remain interior with respect to individual existence, yet determine everything that pertains to this. Much more, that which exists individually is no more or less than (the expression of) these Universal Ideas, without these latter ceasing, for all that, to be in themselves purely intelligible. They are, then, external in so far as determinations implied in the individual existence and, on the other hand, interior in so far as they are intelligible realities. Everything which exists individually emanates from these Ideas, which remain, however, inseparably united to the intellect and could not individually be manifested in such a way as to be removed from the purely intelligible existence, whether it is a question of individual manifestation in time or out of time;[30] for the relation between the individual being and the Universal Idea is always the same, whether or not this being be subject to temporal condition. Only, the Universal Idea assumes in its turn certain conditions pertaining to individual existences following the realities (haqâïq) which define these same existences. Thus for example is the relationship which unites the knowledge and he who knows, or life and he who lives; knowledge and life are intelligible realities, distinct from one another; so, we affirm of God that He knows and lives and we affirm equally of the Angel that he knows and lives, and we say as much of man; in all these cases, the intelligible reality of knowledge or that of life remain the same, and its relationship to he who knows and to he who lives is identical each time; and yet one says of Divine Knowledge that it is eternal, and of man's knowledge that it is ephemeral; there is then, something in this intelligible reality which is ephemeral by its dependence with regard to a (limiting) condition. Now, consider the reciprocal dependence of ideal realities and individual realities:[31] in the same way that knowledge determines he who participates in it – for one calls him knowledgeable – so he who is qualified by knowledge determines in his turn the knowledge, so that it is ephemeral in connection with

[30] According to the language which Ibn 'Arabi uses here, the idea of 'individual existence' (wujûd 'aynî) may be symbolically transposed beyond the formal condition, which is the domain of individuation correctly speaking. Thus, for example, an Angel is not an 'individual' because he does not represent a variant within the interior of a species; however, the argument stated above applies equally to the Angels.

[31] Al-mawjûdâh al-'ayniyah; the existences – or realities – individual or substantial; see preceding note.

[14]

the ephemeral, and eternal in connection with the eternal; and each of these two sides is, in relation to the other, at once determining and determined. It is certain that these Universal Ideas, in spite of their intelligibility, have not, as such, (their own) existence but only a principial existence; likewise, when they apply themselves to individuals they accept the condition (*hukm*) without however assuming thereby distinction or divisibility; they are integrally present in everything qualified by them, like humanity (the quality of man), for example, is present integrally in each particular being of this species without undergoing the distinction nor the number which affects individuals, and without ceasing to be in itself a purely intellectual reality.

Now, as there is a mutual dependence between that which has an individual (or substantial) existence, and that which has not and is, to tell the truth, but a non-existent relationship[32] as such, it is easy to conceive that beings are bound between themselves; for in this case there is always a common denominator, meaning existence as such, while in the former case the mutual relationship exists in spite of the absence of a common denominator.

Without doubt, the ephemeral is not conceivable as such, that is in its ephemeral and relative nature, except in relation to a principle from which it derives its own possibility, so that it has no being in itself, but derives it from another to whom it is tied by its dependence. And it is certain that this principle is in itself necessary, that it is subsistent by itself and independent, in its being, of any other thing. It is this principle, which by its own essence, confers the being to the ephemeral which depends on it.

But since (the principle) demands on its own account the (existence) of the ephemeral (being), this proves itself in this respect as (not only 'possible' but also) 'necessary'. And since the ephemeral depends essentially on its principle it must also appear in the (qualitative) 'form' of the latter in everything that it derives from it, like the 'names' and the qualities, with the exception however of the principial autonomy which is not applicable to the ephemeral being, even though it be 'necessary'; that is, it is necessary by virtue of another, not of itself.

Since the ephemeral being manifests the 'form' of the eternal, it is by the contemplation of the ephemeral that God communicates to us the knowledge of Himself: He says to us (in the Koran) that He shows us His 'signs' in the ephemeral: ('We will show them Our signs to the

[32] This is to say non-manifested.

[15]

horizons and in themselves . . .' XLI, 53). It is from ourselves that we conclude that He is; to Him we attribute no quality without ourselves having that quality with the exception of the principial autonomy. Since we know Him by ourselves and from ourselves, we attribute to Him all that we attribute to ourselves, and it is because of that, again, that the revelation was given by the mouth of the interpreters, (that is to say the prophets) and that God described Himself to us through ourselves. In contemplating Him we contemplate ourselves, and in contemplating ourselves He contemplates Himself, although we are obviously numerous as to the individuals and types; we are united, it is true, in a single and essential reality, but there exists none the less a distinction between individuals, without which, moreover, there would be no multiplicity in the unity.

In the same way, although we are qualified in every respect by the qualities which come from God Himself, there is (between Him and us) certainly a difference, that is to say our dependence towards Him, in so far as He is the Being, and our essential conformity to Him, because of our very possibility; but He is independent of all that which constitutes our indigence. It is in this sense that one should understand eternity without beginning (*al-azal*) and the antiquity (*al-qidam*) of God, which abolishes moreover, the Divine Primacy (*al-awwaliyah*) signifying the passage from non-existence to existence; even though God be the First (*al-awwal*) and the Last (*al-âkhir*) He cannot be called the First in the temporal sense, because then He would in that sense be the Last; but the possibilities of manifestation have no end: they are inexhaustible. If God is called the Last, it means that all reality returns finally to Him after having been brought to us: His quality of the Last is thus essentially His quality of First and inversely. We also know that God has described Himself as 'Exterior' (*al-zâhir*) and as 'Interior' (*al-bâtin*) and that He manifested the world at the same time as interior and exterior, so that we should know the 'interior' aspect (of God) by our own interior, and the 'exterior' by our exterior. In the same way He has described Himself by the qualities of mercy and of anger, and He manifested the world as a place of fear and hope, so that we should fear His anger and hope for His clemency. He has described Himself by Beauty and Majesty and endowed us with a reverent awe (*al-haybah*) and intimacy (*al-uns*). It is thus for everything concerning Him, and by which He has designated Himself. He symbolized these couples of (complementary)

[16]

qualities by the two hands which He held out towards the creation of
Universal Man; this latter reunites in himself all the essential realities
(*haqâiq*) of the world in his totality, just as in each of his individuals.
The world is the apparent, and the representative (of God in it) is the
hidden. It is for this that the Sultan remains invisible and it is in this
sense that God says of Himself that He hides behind the veils of
darkness – which are natural bodies – and the veils of light – which
are subtle spirits;[33] for the world is made of crude (*kathîf*) and of
subtle matter (*latîf*).

(The world) is to itself its own veil and thus cannot see God, due to
the very fact that it sees itself; it can never by itself get rid of its veil,
in spite of knowing that it is attached, by its dependence, to its Creator.
The fact is the world does not participate in the autonomy of the
Essential Being, so much so that it can never conceive Him. In this
respect God remains always unknown, to the intuition as well as to
the contemplation, for the ephemeral has no hold on that (that is to
say the eternal).

When God says to Iblis 'What is it that prevents you from prostrating yourself before that which I have created with My two Hands?',[34]
the mention of two Hands indicates a distinction for Adam; God thus
makes allusion to the union in Adam of the two forms, that is the form
of the world (analogous to the passive Divine Qualities) and the Divine
'form' (analogous to the active Divine Qualities) which are the two
Hands of God.[35] As for Iblis, he is nothing but a fragment of the
world; he did not receive the synthesised nature, by virtue of which
Adam is a representative of God. If Adam had not been manifested
in the 'Form' of the One who entrusted to him His representation
towards the others, he would not be His representative; and if he did
not contain all that which is needed by the herd that he has to guard –
it is on him that this herd depends, and he must suffice to all their
needs – he would not be representing God for the other (creatures).

The representation of God belongs only to the Universal Man,
whose exterior form is created of realities (*haqâiq*) and of the forms of

[33] According to the word of the Prophet: 'God hides Himself by seventy
thousand veils of light and darkness; if He lifted them, the brilliance of His face
would consume whomsoever looked at It.'

[34] Koran XXXVIII, 75,

[35] The symbolism of the two hands of God is found again in the Kabbala,
particularly in the Zohar, where they are compared to the Heaven and the Earth
in so far as the active and passive principles of the manifestation.

the world, and whose interior form corresponds to the 'Form' of God (that is to say to the 'total' of the Divine Names and Qualities). Because of that God has said of him 'I am his hearing and his sight'; He did not say 'his eye and his ear', but distinguished the two 'forms', one from the other.[36]

It is the same for all beings of this world with regard to each their own (transcendant) reality; however, no being contains the synthesis similar to the one which distinguishes the Representative and it is only by this synthesis that this one surpasses the others. If God did not penetrate existence by His 'form'[37] the world would not be; in the same way as individuals would not be determined if they had not the Universal Ideas. According to this Truth, the existence of the world resides in its dependence with regard to God. In reality each depends (on the other: the 'Divine Form' on that of the world and inversely); nothing is independent (of the other); this is the pure truth; we are not expressing ourselves in metaphors. On the other hand when I speak of that which is absolutely independent thou wilt know what I mean by it (that is to say the infinite unconditioned Essence). Each, (the 'Divine Form' as the world), is then tied one to the other and one cannot be separated from the other; understand well what I tell thee!

Now, thou knowest the spiritual meaning of the creation of Adam's body, that is to say of his apparent form, and of the creation of his spirit, which is his interior 'form'. Adam is, then, at the same time, God and creature. And thou hast understood that which is his (cosmic) rank that is to say the synthesis (of all the cosmic qualities), synthesis by virtue of which he is the Representative of God.

Adam is the 'unique Spirit' (an-nafs al-wâhidah) from which was created the human species according to the Divine Word, (in the

[36] According to the divine Word, revealed through the mouth of the Prophet (hadîth qudsî): 'My servant can only approach Me with something which pleases Me more than that which I impose on him. My servant approaches Me ceaselessly by free acts until I love him; and when I love him, I am the hearing by which he hears, the sight by which he sees, the hand with which he takes hold, and the foot with which he walks: If he prays to Me, I give to him certainly, and if he looks for My help, I help him certainly' (Cited by al-Bukhârî according to Abu Hurayrah).

[37] The expression 'form' is analogous here to the peripatetic notion of 'forma' (eidos), that is to say the qualitative mark; we remember that the quality can be transposed into the pure universal. With reference to the word of the Prophet: 'God created Adam in His "form" (sûrah).' Sufism calls 'divine Form' the total of perfect Qualities by which God reveals Himself in the Universe.

Koran); 'O you, mankind, fear your Lord, who hath created you out of one soul and out of him created his wife, and from them hath deployed many men and women' (IV, 1). The words 'fear your Lord' signify: make of your apparent form a safeguard for your Lord, and make of your interior – that is to say of your Lord – a safeguard for yourselves; every act (or every Divine Order) consists in blame or in praise (in negation or in affirmation); then be His safeguard in the blame (that is to say as limited creatures) and take Him for safeguard in the praise,[38] so that you have, amongst all beings, the most just attitude (towards God).

After He had created him, God showed Adam all that He had put into him; and He held it all in His two Hands: one containing the world and the other Adam and his descendants, then He showed these the ranks that they occupied in the interior of Adam.[39]

Since God made me see that which He put in the primordial generator I have transcribed in this book the portion which was assigned to me, and not everything that I have realised; for that, no book in the present world could contain. But, among the things that I have contemplated and which could be transcribed in this book, as far as was assigned to me by God's Messenger – May Benediction and Peace be on him! – was the Divine Wisdom in the Word of Adam: it is that which this chapter discusses.

[38] According to Al-Qashâni: Take Him as safeguard in praise by attributing the limitations to you and all the positive qualities to God, conforming to the Koranic word: 'What ever good befalleth thee it is from God, and whatever evil befalleth thee, it is from thyself'. Koran IV, 81.

[39] According to the Koranic saying: 'And when thy Lord drew forth their seed from the loins of the sons of Adam, and took them to witness against themselves, saying: Am I not your Lord? They answered: Yea: we do bear witness. This was done lest ye should say, at the day of resurrection, Verily we had neglected this'. Koran VII, 171.

Of the Wisdom of the Divine Inspiration
(al-hikmat an-nafathiyah)
in the Word of Seth

KNOW that the gifts and favours (of God),[1] that are lavished on this world through the mediation of creatures or without their mediation, distinguish themselves for men of spiritual leaning (adh-dhawq), by essential gifts (like immediate Knowledge) and by gifts which proceed from the Divine Names (that is to say the Divine aspects such as Beauty, Goodness, Life, etc.). Furthermore they differ according to whether they are received as the result of a direct request or if they correspond to undetermined requests, or again if they are received without any request at all, and that independently of their distinction between essential gifts, and gifts conforming to the Divine Names. It is a determined request if someone says: 'Oh Lord, give me such and such a thing' and if his aim is only of this thing. A request which is not determined, on the other hand, is that of a man who prays: 'Oh Lord, give me that which is for my good, for all parts, subtle and corporal, of my being', without thinking of any one thing in particular.

As for those who ask, they can be divided into two groups; the one obeys a natural impulse to hurry the attainment (of the thing that they desire) – for 'man was created impatient'[2] and the others ask because they know that there are, near to God, things which, according to the

---

[1] Seth was the gift of God for Adam. By his birth, the murder of Abel was compensated and the broken order re-established. As first prophet amongst the descendants of Adam, he was the true son, corporal and spiritual, of his father. But, as Ibn 'Arabi writes in the chapter on Enoch, 'the son is the secret of his father', that is to say that he symbolizes the interior aspect. Conforming to this symbolism, this chapter implies a spiritual perspective contrary to that which the preceding chapter represented. Whereas the chapter on Adam described the universal manifestation of God, or the 'vision' that God has of Himself in Universal Man, the chapter on Seth has for its subject the interior revelation of God or the knowledge which man has of himself in the divine 'mirror'.

[2] Koran XVII, 12.

Divine foreknowledge, can only be obtained by virtue of a request; so, then, they say to themselves : 'perhaps that which I ask of God is of this sort'. Their requests take into consideration, in a global manner, the possible methods of the Divine Order; they do not know what the Divine Science implies, nor that which will result from their own pre-disposition (*isti'dâd*) to receive; for it is one of the most difficult things to know the predisposition of a being at each single instant (of his life); moreover, if he had not been predisposed to such a request, he would not request it. As for the contemplatives who do not know their pre-disposition, they recognize it, in the best cases, at the very instant they live; for by the state of their presence (*hudûr*) (with God) they know that which God gives them at that instant; and know they receive it only by reason of their predisposition. They are divided, in their turn, into two categories : the ones who know their predispositions from what they have received; the others who know what they will receive because of their predisposition; and it is this latter knowledge which is the most perfect within this group.

Belonging to this category are those who ask, not to accelerate the obtaining of a gift, nor to take into consideration the possible modes (of the Divine favour) but to conform to the Divine Order expressed by the Word : 'Ask me and I will answer you !' It is the adorer (*al-'abd*) 'par excellence'; when he asks, his desire does not attach itself to the thing asked for, whether it be determined or not, but looks to conform to the order of his Lord. When his spiritual state requires abandon and tranquillity, he is quiet; thus, Job and others were tried, and did not ask God to comfort them in their trial, until their spiritual state re-quired, at a certain moment, that they should ask that it should be lifted; then they asked, and God comforted them.

That the granting of a request be immediate or that it be deferred depends on the measure (*qadr*) predestined by God; if the demand is made at the moment predestined for the answer, this is immediate, and if the granting is predestined for a subsequent time, be it in this world or beyond, the answer will be adjourned; I mean the effective granting of the request, not the Divine reply : 'I am present' (which is always immediate); understand me well !

As for the second category of gifts, of which we were saying that they are received without request, we must state precisely what we mean by request : prayer expressed in words; for in principle there must always be a request whether it be articulated, consists of a spiritual state (*hâl*) or, whether it results simply from the (intimate) predisposition of the being. In the same way, to praise God signifies, if necessary, to pronounce praise towards Him; but in the spiritual sense, this praise is necessarily determined by a spiritual state, for that which incites thee to praise God is (in compliance) with a Divine Name, expressing an activity of God or an aspect of His Transcendence. As for his predisposition, the individual being is not conscious of it, that which he feels is the state (*al-hâl*), for he knows that which incites him (to praise or request); the predisposition remains the most hidden thing.

That which prevents some from asking, is knowing that God has decided their destiny for all eternity; they have prepared their abode (that is to say their soul) to receive that which will come from Him, and they have divested themselves of their ego (*an-nafs*) and of their individual existence. Amongst these there is he who knows that the knowledge God has of him, in each of his states, is identifiable to that which he is himself in his state of (principial) immutability before his manifestation; and he knows that God will give him nothing that does not result from this essence (*al-'ayn*), that he is himself in his permanent principial state. He knows then from whence the Divine Knowledge comes towards himself. No other category from amongst those who know God is superior to those who realize thus the mystery of the predisposition. They are divided in their turn, into two groups: there are those who realize this in a general manner, others in a distinct manner; the latter occupy the superior rank; for he who has a distinct knowledge of that which is in question realizes that which the Divine Knowledge implies towards him, be it that God reveals to him that which, in the matter of knowledge, results from his own essence (*'aynuh*), be it that He reveals directly His own immutable essence (*al-'ayn aththâbitah*) and endless unfolding of the states derived from it. It is this latter gnostic who occupies the superior rank, for in his knowledge of himself he adopts the Divine point of view, the object of his knowledge being the same as the object of Divine Knowledge. However, when one considers this identification (of the knowledge that the contemplative has of the Divine Knowledge) on the individual side, it seems like a Divine aid predestined to this individual in virtue of certain contents in his immutable essence, contents that this being will recognise as soon as God lets him see them; for when God shows him the contents of his immutable essence, which, itself, receives directly from the Being,[3]

[3] The immutable essence or archetype has not a being as such, for it is but a

that, evidently, surpasses the faculties of a creature as such; for he is incapable of appropriating the Divine Knowledge which is applied to those archetypes (al-a'yân ath-thâbitah) in their state of non-existence ('udum), these archetypes being but the pure, essential relations (nisab dhâtiyah) without proper forms. It is in this respect (that is to say, because of the immeasurable magnitude of the Divine Knowledge and of individual knowledge) that we say of this identification (of the Divine Knowledge) that it represents a Divine aid predestined to a certain individual.

It is in this same respect that one must understand the Divine Word '(We will try you,) until We know . . .'[4] (as if God did not know in advance what all creatures will do) which is an expression rigorously adequate, contrarily to that which is believed by those who do not drink from this source; for the transcendence of God affirms itself the most perfectly by the fact that Knowledge appears temporal by its relation (to something temporal, just as it appears eternal in connection with an eternal object). That is the most universal aspect that a theologian can logically conceive in this matter, unless he considers the Divine Science as distinct from the Essence and attributes the relativity to the Science in so far as it differs from the Essence. From (this last point of view), he is distinguishable moreover from the real knowers of God, gifted with intuition (kashf) and realizing the Being (al-wujûd).

But let us return now to the distinction between the (Divine) gifts and the essential gifts and gifts conforming to the Names. As for those which are favours and essential gifts, they are only granted by virtue of a Divine revelation (or irradiation; (tajallî)); now, the Essence only reveals itself in the 'form' of the predisposition of the individual who receives this revelation; never does anything else happen. From that time, the subject receiving the essential revelation will see his own 'form' in the 'mirror' of God; he will not see God – it is impossible that he should see Him, – knowing all the while that he sees only his own 'form' by virtue of this Divine mirror. This is completely analogous to that which takes place in a corporal mirror : in contemplating the forms in it, thou dost not see the mirror, at the same time knowing

---

non-manifested possibility contained in the Divine Essence. It is in an entirely symbolic manner that the archetype can be considered as a receptacle (qâbil) or a 'mould', as if 'opposing itself' to the Divine Being. See also the beginning of the chapter on Adam.

4 Koran XLVII, 31.

that thou seest these forms – or thine own form – only by virtue of the mirror.[5] This phenomenon God has manifested as a symbol particularly appropriate to His essential revelation, so that he to whom He reveals Himself knows that he does not see Him; there exists no symbol more direct and more conforming to the contemplation and the revelation in question.[6] Try, then, thyself, to see the body of the mirror as well as looking at the form that it reflects; thou wilt never see it at the same time. This is so true that certain people, observing this law of reflected forms in mirrors (corporal or spiritual), have claimed that the reflected form interposes itself between the view of the contemplative and the mirror itself; and that is all that they have grasped of the highest sense in the domain of spiritual knowledge; but in reality it is as we have just said (in knowing that the reflected form does not essentially hide the mirror, but that the mirror manifests it). Moreover we have already explained this point in our book 'Revelations from Mecca' (al-Futûhât al-Makkiyah). If thou dost appreciate that, thou dost appreciate the extreme limit that a creature as such can attain (in 'objective' knowledge); do not aspire, then, beyond that and do not tire thy soul by surpassing this degree, for there is nothing there, in principle and definitely, but pure non-existence (the Essence being non-manifest). God, then, is the mirror in which thou seest thyself as thou art His mirror in which He contemplates His Names.[7] Now these are none other than Himself, so that reality reverses itself and becomes ambiguous. Some of us imply ignorance in their knowledge (of God) and cite in this respect the word (of Calif Abu Bakr): 'To realize that one is powerless to know the Knowledge is already knowledge'. But amongst us there is one who knows (truly), and does not say these

---

[5] According to the Advaïtic terminology, God is the absolute Subject – or the Witness (sâkshin) – which will never become the 'Object' of knowledge. It is in Him or from Him that everything is perceived, while He remains there always incomprehensible in the background. 'The looks do not reach Him, but it is He who reaches the looks' says the Koran, VI, 103.

[6] In his 'Divine Comedy' Dante causes Adam to say when he explains to him his intemporal vision of the nature of the beings in God:

'Perch'io la veggio nel verace speglio,
Che fa di se pareglio all'altre cose,
E nulla face lui di se pareglio,'

Paradise XXVI, 106 ss.

(Because I see it in the truthful mirror
Which makes of itself the equal of other things,
And nothing makes of itself the equal).

[7] Certain editions of the text add: 'and their principles'.

[24]

words; his knowledge does not imply a powerlessness to know, it implies the inexpressible; it is this latter that has the most perfect consciousness of God.

Now, this knowledge is given only to the Seal of God's Messengers (*khâtim ar-rusûl*);[8] and to the Seal of the Saints (*khâtim al-awliyâ*);[9] none of the prophets and messengers[10] imbibe it anywhere else than in the tabernacle (*mishkât*)[11] of the messenger who is their seal. Again, none of the saints imbibes it elsewhere than in the tabernacle of the saint who is their seal; so that the messengers also imbibe this knowledge, in so far as they imbibe it, in the tabernacle of the Seal of the Saints; for the function of the messenger of God and that of the prophet – I mean the prophetic function in so far as it brings about the promulgation of a sacred law – ceases, whereas saintliness never ceases; so, the messengers only receive this knowledge because they are also saints, and solely from the tabernacle of the Seal of Saints.[12]

[8] Title of the Prophet Muhammed as the last of the legislators inspired by God.

[9] The role of 'Seal of the Prophets' corresponds to an apparent cyclic function, whereas the function of the 'Seal of Saints' is necessarily intemporal and hidden; it represents the prototype of the spirituality, independently of all 'mission' (*risâlah*).

[10] Every 'messenger' (*rasûl*) is prophet (*nabî*) by his degree of inspiration; however, only the prophet who promulgates a new sacred law is called 'messenger'.

[11] The symbolism of the tabernacle (*al-mishkât*) or of the 'Niche of Light' refers to the following Koranic passage: 'God is the Light of heaven and of earth: the symbol of His light is as a tabernacle (or niche), wherein there is a lamp, and the lamp enclosed in a case of glass; the glass appears as it were a shining star. It is lighted (with the oil) of a blessed olive tree, which is neither of the east, nor of the west, and whose oil is almost luminous, although no fire touched it. Light upon light. God will direct unto His light whom He pleaseth; and God proposes parables unto men; and God knoweth all things.' (Koran XXIV, 35). In Sufism, the 'Niche of Light' is identified to the deepest interior of Universal Man.

[12] In the *Futûhât al-Makkiyah*, Ibn Arabi speaks also of the 'Seal of the Sainthood of the Prophets and the Messengers' (IV, 57); by that he means Christ at the time of his second coming before the end of time. This function, which may seem contradictory in itself is explained in the following manner: the 'messenger' who 'will seal' the present great cycle of humanity and will save the chosen ones by causing them to pass into the future cycle, evidently cannot carry a new sacred law, which would only have a sense for a collectivity having to exist as such, but will, on the other hand bring forth the intrinsic truths common to all the traditional forms; he will address himself, then, to humanity in its entirety, which he will be able to do only by situating himself to a certain degree on an esoteric plane, which is that of the contemplative saint (*al-walî*); he will be at once prophet and messenger in an implicit manner, because of his

Since it is thus (for the messengers and for the prophets) how would it be different for the other saints? And this is true, although the Seal of the Saints conforms himself to the sacred Law given by the Seal of the Prophets; that does not prejudice his spiritual rank and takes away nothing from that which we have just said; for it is possible that it is inferior from a certain point of view, at the same time being superior from another point of view. What we mean by that can be found confirmed, moreover, in the history of our religion, by the preference (due to an ulterior revelation) of the judgement of Omar (to that of the Prophet) on that which concerned the treatment of the prisoners after the battle of Badr, (the Prophet having wished to accept a ransom for them, whereas Omar advised liberating them or condemning them); in the same way it manifests itself in the episode concerning the fertilization of a date palm (where the advice of the Prophet failed, which led him to say : 'You are more expert than I in the affairs of your world down here'). It is not necessary that the perfect surpasses the others in every respect; but spiritual men consider only the superiority with regard to the Knowledge of God; as for ephemeral existences, their mind does not at all dwell on it. – Realize then, that which we have just revealed.

When the Prophet compared the prophetic function to a brick wall almost finished and which needed only one more brick, he identified himself with this last brick.[13] He saw, then, as he said, only the place for a single brick to fill. But, the Seal of the Saints will have an analogous vision; only, he will perceive, in that which the Prophet symbolized by the unfinished wall, the place for two bricks to fill; the bricks from which the wall is built will appear to him of gold and silver, and the two bricks still needed to complete the construction will be a brick

---

eminently cyclic function, but he will be explicitly a 'saint', whereas the opposite took place for almost all the preceding prophets. Let us remark here that Christ, of whom the Koran speaks as a 'messenger' (rasûl) manifested already at the time of his first coming, such an 'extraversion' of 'saintliness' (wilâyâ) and of esotericism, which made of him, moreover, in the eyes of the Sufis the model of saint 'par excellence'; and it is necessary that it be thus so that there is, outside any question of cosmological order, a veritable spiritual identity between Christ preceding Muhammed and Christ 're-descended' at the end of time. – In the same passage of the Futûhât, Ibn 'Arabi talks of the 'Seal of the Muhammedan Sainthood' which he distinguishes from the 'Seal of Sainthood of the Prophets and Messengers'; it is the former which is also the 'Seal of Universal Sainthood'.

[13] 'My figure among the Prophets is thus: a man built a wall, he has finished it, except that it needs one more brick; it is I who am this brick; after me there will be no more messengers (rasûl) nor prophets (nabî)' (Hadîth).

of gold and a brick of silver; and the Seal of the Saints will see himself corresponding to the place which these two bricks are needed to fill. The reason that he sees himself in the form of two bricks is that he adheres externally to the law given by the Seal of the Messengers – that which corresponds to the silver brick, and that he imbibes internally in God exactly that which, according to his apparent form, presents itself as an adhesion to the law which preceded him; for he sees necessarily the Divine Order (*al-amr*) as it is – and it is that which corresponds to the golden brick, symbol of his internal nature – since the Seal of the Saints imbibes at the same source as that from which the Angel imbibed, who inspired the Messenger of God[14] – If thou understandeth that to which I allude, thou hast reached the fully efficacious knowledge. All prophets, without exception, since Adam until the last, imbibe, then (their light) in the tabernacle of the Seal of the Prophets; if the clay of the latter has been formed only after the others, it is no less present by its spiritual reality, conforming to the word (of Muhammed): 'I was a prophet when Adam was still between water and clay'. Every other prophet does not become one until he is awakened to his function. In the same way, the Seal of the Saints was saintly 'when Adam was still between water and clay', whereas the other saints only became saints after having realized the conditions of saintliness, which are the assimilation of the Divine Qualities flowing from the aspect of God which are expressed by His Names, the Saint, the Adored (*al-walî, al-hamîd*, this latter indicating the prototype of the positive qualities of the created one). The Seal of the Messengers is connected, then, in respect of his saintliness, to the Seal of the Saints, in the same way as the other messengers and prophets are connected to him. For he is himself simultaneously the saint (*al-walî*), the messenger (*ar-rasûl*) and the prophet (*an-nabî*). As for the Seal of the Saints, he is the saint, the heir, (*al-wârith*) who imbibes in the origin, the one who contemplates all ranks ...

Let us come now to the gifts which flow from the Divine Names: the Mercy (*rahmah*) which God lavishes on His creatures runs wholly through the Divine Names: it is, on the one hand of pure mercy, like everything that is licit from nourishment and natural pleasures, and which is not tainted with blame at the day of resurrection (conforming to the Koranic word: 'Say, who then would render illicit the beauty which God manifested for His servants and the lawful things of

[14] C.f. The word of Christ 'Before Abraham was, I was' (St. John VIII, 58.)

nourishment; say : they are for those who believe, in this world, and will not be subject to reproach on the day of resurrection . . .') – and it is these gifts which flow from the name *ar-rahmân*, – on the other hand of mercy which is mixed (with punishment), like medicine which is disagreeable to take, but which is followed by relief. Such are the Divine gifts, for God (in His personal or qualified aspect) never gives except through the intermediary of one of the guardians of the temple which are His Names. Thus, God sometimes gratifies the servant by mediation of the name the Compassionate (*ar-rahmân*), and it is then that the gift is free from any mixture which would be momentarily contrary to the nature of he who receives it, or which would contradict the intention or anything else (of the petitioner); sometimes, He gives by the mediation of the Name the Vast (*al-wâsi*), lavishing His gifts in a global manner, or He gives by the mediation of the Name of the Wise (*al-hakîm*) judging by that which is salutory (for the servant) at the given moment, or by the mediation of the Name of He who gives freely (*al-wahhâb*), giving that which is good without the one who receives it, by virtue of this Name, needing to compensate for it by actions of grace or merit : or He gives by the Name of He who establishes the order (*al-jabbâr*), considering the cosmic environment and that which is necessary to it, or by the Name of the Forgiver (*al-ghaffâr*), considering the state of he who receives the forgiveness : if he finds himself in a state which deserves punishment, He protects him from this punishment, and if he finds himself in a state which would not deserve punishment He protects him from a state which would deserve it, and it is in this sense that the Servant (saint) is said to be protected or safeguarded from sin. The giver is always God, in the sense that it is He the treasurer of all possibilities and that He only produces according to a predestined measure and by the hand of a Name concerning that possibility. Thus, He gives to everything its own constitution by virtue of His name the Just (*al-'adl*) and of its brothers (like the Arbitrator : (*al-hakam*), He who rules : (*al-wâlî*), the Victorious : (*al-qahhâr*) etc.).

Although the Divine Names may be infinite as to their multitude – for one knows them by that which flows from them and which is equally unlimited – they are none the less reducible to a definite number of 'roots' which are the 'mothers' of the Divine Names or the (Divine) Presences integrating the Names. In truth, there is but one single essential Reality (*haqîqah*) which assumes all the relations and associations which one ascribes to it by the Divine Names. Now, this essential Reality causes each of these Names which manifest themselves indefinitely to contain an essential truth by which it distinguishes itself from the other Names; it is this distinctive truth, and not that which it has in common with the others, which is the proper determination of the Name. It is in the same way that the Divine gifts distinguish themselves one from another by their personal nature, although they come from the same source – it is moreover evident that this one is not that one – the reason being precisely the distinction of the Divine Names. Because of His infinity, there is in the Divine Presence absolutely nothing that repeats itself – and that is a fundamental truth.

This is the science of Seth, Peace on him! His spirit communicates it to all spirits whom He has proffered something, with the exception however of the spirit of the Seal which receives this knowledge directly from God, and not by the mediation of some other spirit; much more, it is from the Seal's own spirit that this knowledge flows to each spirit, even though each may not be conscious of it while it exists in corporal form. In its essential reality, and in its purely spiritual function, it knows, then, directly, all that it is ignorant of by its corporal constitution. It is, then, at the same time knowing and ignorant, and one can attribute to it apparently contrary qualities, in the same way that its (Divine) principle, which is its very essence (*'aynuh*), is at once terrible and generous, the First and the Last. It knows then and it does not know, at the same time, it perceives and it does not perceive, it contemplates and yet does not contemplate.

It is by virtue of this science that Seth received his name which signifies the gift, that is to say the gift of God, for he holds the key of the divine gift according to the various ways and in all aspects. It is thus, because God made of Seth a present for Adam, and he was the first gratuitous gift that God made (that is to say the first gift that did not demand from he who received it some sort of compensation) and it is from Adam himself that it came, for the son is the secret reality of his generator; it is from him that he issues and to him that he returns, so he does not, then, befall to him like something unknown to him. It is this which will be understood by he who sees things from a Divine point of view. Moreover, every gift in the entire universe, is manifested according to this law: nobody receives something from God, (that is to say) nobody receives anything which does not come from himself, whatever may be the unpredictable variation of the forms. But few

[29]

know this, some only of the initiated know this spiritual law. So if thou dost encounter anyone who knows it, thou mayest have confidence in him, for such a man is the pure quintessence and the chosen amongst the chosen of the spiritual men.

Every time that an intuitive person contemplates a form which communicates to him new knowledge which he had not been able previously to comprehend, this form will be an expression of his own essence (*'ayn*) and nothing unknown to him. It is from the tree of his own soul that he gathers the fruit of his culture, in the same way that his image, reflected by a polished surface is nothing but himself although the place of reflection – or the Divine Presence – which returns to him his own form, provokes the inversions following the essential Truth inherent in such a (Divine) Presence.[15] It is thus that, in the case of a concrete mirror, it so happens that it reflects things according to their real proportions, the large as the large, the small as the small, the lying down as the lying down, the moving as movement, but also (following the constitution or following the perspective) it can reverse the proportions; in the same way it is possible that a mirror reflects things without the usual reversions, showing the right side of the contemplative from his right side, whereas generally the right side of the reflected image is found opposite the left side of he who is looking at himself; there can, therefore, be exceptions to the rule, like in the case where the proportions are reversed; and all that applies equally to the diverse ways of the (Divine) Presence, in which the revelation takes place (of the essential 'form' of the contemplative) and which we have compared to the mirror.

He who knows his pre-disposition, knows from himself what he will receive. On the other hand, he who knows what he receives does not necessarily know his pre-disposition, unless he knows it after having received, be it only in a global manner.

---

[15] The contemplative states may be conceived as Divine 'Presences' (*hadarât*) or as diverse modalities of the single Presence of God. There is an indefinite number of Divine Presences; however, one distinguishes generally, five fundamental Presences, and these according to the diverse 'schemes' of which we will mention here the following: To the 'Presence of the Absolute non-manifestation' (*hadarât al-ghayb al mutlaq*) is opposed – not in the Divine Reality but according to a point of view strictly human and provisional – the 'Presence of the achieved manifestation' (*hadarât ash-shahâdat al-mutlaqah*), that is to say the 'objective' world. Between these two 'Presences' is situated the 'Presence' of the 'relative non-manifestation' (*hadarât al-ghayb al mudâfî*) which is subdivided in its turn into two distinct cosmic regions, of which one, that of the supraformal

Certain thinkers, intellectually feeble, starting from the dogma that God does all that He wishes, have declared it admissible that God should act contrarily to principles and contrarily to that which is the Reality (al-amr) in itself (that is in its principial state – as if the manifestation of God did not proceed from the possibilities eternally present in the Divine Being and in the Universal Intellect). From this, they have gone so far as to deny the possibility as such and to accept (as logical and ontological categories) only the absolute necessity (that is the very 'existence' of God) and the necessity through others (that is to say the relative necessity). But the wise man admits the possibility, of which he knows the ontological rank : obviously, possibility (as such) is not the possible (in the sense of that which could exist or could not exist) and how could it be so since it is essentially necessary because of a (principle) other than itself. But in the end, from whence then comes this distinction between it and its principle which makes it necessary (and by which it constitutes precisely a possibility of manifestation)? But nobody knows the distinction in question except those who know God !

It is in the traces of Seth that the last of the human species will be manifested; he will inherit the mysteries of Seth; there will be no other begotten after him, so that he will be the Seal of the begotten, (as Seth had been the first Saint). With him will be born a sister; she will emerge before him (whereas the first woman was manifested after the first man); and he will follow her, having his head at the feet of his sister. The place of his birth will be in China (the country furthest east); and he will speak the language of the country of his birth. At that time, sterility will spread throughout woman and man; so that there will be much cohabitation without generation. He will call the people to God, but there will be no response. When God has taken his spirit and He has taken the last believer of that time, those who survive will be like brutes, and they will not distinguish the licit from the illicit; they will react according to their purely natural inclinations, following desire, independently of reason and law; and it is on them that the last hour will rise.

---

existence (al-jabarût) is the closest to the Absolute 'non-manifestation', whereas the other, that of the world of subtle forms ('âlem al-mithâl) approaches the 'achieved manifestation'. These four Presences are all englobed by a fifth, the total 'Presence' (al-hadarât al-jâm'iyah) which is identified with Universal Man (al-insân al-kâmil). – We will add that this distinction of the 'Presences' is in conformity with a perspective in some ways 'practical', that is to say connected with the contemplative way and not to the pure metaphysical doctrine.

Extract from the Chapter:
Of the Wisdom of the Transcendence
(al-hikmat as-subûhiyah)
in the Word of Noah

FOR those who know the Divine Truths (ahl al-haqâïq), to affirm (unilaterally) that God is incomparable to things, is precisely to limit and render conditional the conception of the Divine Reality (for one excludes, thus, the quality of things); he who denies all resemblance to God, without alienating himself from this exclusive point of view, manifests either ignorance, or lack of 'tact' (adab). The exoterist who insists uniquely on the Divine transcendence (at-tanzîh) (to the exclusion of the immanence) (at-tashbîh) slanders God and His messengers – Divine Benediction be on them! – without being aware of it; imagining that he reaches the target, he strikes everything else aside; for he is of those who accept only one part of the Divine revelation and rejects the other.[1]

One knows that the Scriptures revealed as common law (sharî 'ah) express themselves, in talking of God, in such a way that the majority of men understand the most obvious meaning, whereas the elite under-

---

[1] The Islamic theology, like that of the Greek fathers, distinguishes two ways of envisaging the Divine Nature: the 'exaltation' or the 'separation' (at-tanzîh), which denies all similitude of God with things and affirms His transcendence, and the 'comparison' or the 'analogy' (at-tasbîh) which, on the contrary describes God by means of symbols and manifests thereby His immanence in things. The two perspectives are in reality complementary, and the doctrinal error 'par excellence' consists in maintaining one of them to the exclusion of the other; the 'separation' is superior to the 'comparison' in the sense that the negation of all limitative determination, so the negation of all negation, is the most universal affirmation; however the unilateral 'separation' succeeds in excluding the world of Divine Nature and then to limit this in opposing God and the world; as for the point of view of the 'comparison', it is theoretically inferior to the former, but superior in its contemplative realization, since it corresponds to the direct ascent of the uncreated in the created; it implies in its turn the danger of limiting the Divine Nature.

[32]

stand all the meanings, so as to know the whole significance included in each word conforming to the rules of the language employed.[2]

For God manifests Himself in every creature in a particular way. It is He who reveals Himself in every meaning, and it is He who remains hidden to all understanding, except for he who recognizes in the world the 'form'[3] and the aseity (*huwiyah*) of God, and (who sees the world as) the Divine Name the Apparent (*az-zâhir*). In the same way, one conceives God conceptually as the inherent spirit in all manifestation, so that He is the Interior (*al-bâtin*) in this respect, and He is to every form manifested in this world, the spirit ruling the corporal form which depends on it. The logical definition of man, for example, includes his exterior as well as his interior; and it is the same for every definable thing. As for God, He 'defines' Himself by the sum of all possible 'definitions';[4] but, the 'forms' of the world are indefinite, one could not understand them all, nor know the logical definition of each, except in so far as they fit into the definition of world (or microcosm) given as such. In this way, one cannot know the logical 'form' of God, since one would know it only by knowing the definition of all 'forms', which is an impossibility; to 'define' God, then, is not possible.

In the same way, he who compares God without affirming at the same time His incomparability, attributes to Him limits, and does not recognise Him. But he who unites in his knowledge of God the point of view of the transcendence with that of the immanence, and attributes to God the two 'aspects' globally – for it is impossible to conceive them in detail, in the same way as one could not embrace all the 'forms' of the universe – knows Him truly, that is to say, that he knows Him globally, not distinctively, just as man knows himself globally and not distinctively; and it is for that, moreover, that the Prophet links the knowledge of God to that of oneself, saying : 'he who knows himself, knows his Lord'. On the other hand, God says in the Koran : 'We will show them Our signs unto the horizons' – meaning the exterior world – 'and in themselves' – in thine essence – 'until it becomes evident to them that (all) is God (*al-haqq*)' (XLI, 53) – in this

---

[2] The archaic languages, such as Arabic, contain a plurality of sense in a single expression.

[3] That is to say the total of the Divine Qualities.

[4] This manner of expressing oneself is intentionally paradoxical; in fact the Divine Qualities could not be 'defined' in the proper sense of the term, any more than they could be limited. In the same way, the expression 'form', in the following passages, must be transposed.

sense that thou art His form and that He is thy spirit, so that thou art (in thy totality) for Him that which the corporal form is for thee, and He is to thee that which is the spirit which rules the form of thy body.

Thy definition implies at the same time thy exterior and thy interior reality : for the (corporal) form which remains, when the spirit which governed it has left it, it is no longer a man; one speaks of it as of a form having a human appearance, but which is not distinguishable (essentially) from a form made of wood or stone, and which takes the name man by the extension of the term, and not in its proper sense. But, from the forms of the world, God can never separate Himself (for then they would cease to exist), so that they are necessarily included in the 'definition' of the Divinity (*ulûhiyah*), whereas the exterior form of man is defined only accidentally, so long as he is in this life. In the same way that the exterior form of man 'praises by his tongue' his spirit and his soul which rule it, so the forms of the world 'glorify' God, although we do not understand their praise (according to the Koran : 'there is nothing which does not glorify Him, but you do not understand their praise') (xvii 44), and that because we do not embrace every form of this world. Every one of them is a tongue which pronounces the praise of God; and that is why (the Koran) says, 'Praise be to God, Lord of all of the Universes' (i, 2) which means that all praise refers finally to Him. So that He is at once He who praises and He who is praised. If thou dost affirm the Divine transcendence, thou dost condition (the conception of God) and if thou does affirm His immanence, thou dost limit Him; but if thou dost affirm simultaneously the one and the other point of view, thou wilt be exempt from error and be a model of knowledge.

He who affirms the duality (of God and the world) falls in the error of associating something with God; and he who affirms the singularity of God (excluding from his Reality everything which manifests itself in multiplicity) commits the fault of confining Him to a (rational) unity. Be careful of comparison when thou dost envisage duality; and be careful not to separate the Divinity when thou dost envisage Unity !

Thou art not Him; and yet thou art Him; thou wilt see Him in the essence of things, sovereign and conditioned at the same time.[5]

[5] We have translated here the first part of the chapter on Noah, because the rest, an exegesis of Koranic passages concerning the story of this patriarch, stresses the verbal symbolism which would be impossible to translate into another language. Let us, all the same, recapitulate some aspects of this chapter. Accord-

Extracts from the Chapter:
Of the Saintly Wisdom *(al-hikmat al-quddûsiyah)*
in the Word of Enoch (Idris)

ONE of the Names of Perfection of God is the Eminent *(al-'âlî)*. But with regard to what then is He Eminent, since there is only Him? (The relative existences being unable to be taken as a term of comparison with the Supreme Being). Is He essentially the Eminent or is He that with respect to something else? Now, everything is nothing but Him. Therefore He is the Eminent in Himself. On the other hand, since He is the Being of all that exists, the ephemeral existences are, they too, eminent in their essence, for they are essentially identical to Him.

God is the Eminent without relativity; for the essences (of beings) *(al-a'yân)* which are (in themselves) nothing but non-existence *('adam)*, and which are immutable in this state, have not even smelt the odour of existence *(al-wujûd)*;[1] they stay just as they were, in spite of the multiplicity of the forms in the manifested realities. As for the essential

---

ing to the Koran, Noah revealed the unity and the divine transcendence to an idolatrous people. The idolatory results from a unilateral affirmation of the point of view of 'comparison', or of immanence, to the detriment of the Divine transcendence. According to Ibn 'Arabi, the idols adored by the people who perished in the flood, were none other than the personifications of the Divine 'Names' – of 'Aspects' of the Supreme Being – of which the people had finally forgotten the transcendent reality and consequently the essential unity. The error of the idolators caused the predication of Noah, in the sense that he had to affirm the transcendence and was prevented from affirming explicitly the immanence of God; for the cosmic function of the Prophet requires the counterbalancing of the unbalanced and finds itself bound in some ways by this law. On their side, the idolators remained resolutely by the truth which their error deformed, so that the predication of Noah drove them back even more on their attitude. All the prophetic revelation produces, thus, by that which it denies and by that which it affirms, oppositions on the terrestrial plane and finally calls, in the economy of traditional forms, complementary affirmations and negations.

[1] An-Nâbulusî comments: '. . . because they are but pure possibilities, which as such will never pass into the state of "necessary being".'

determination (*al-'ayn*) of the Being, it is unique among all and in all. The multiplicity exists only in the Names, which are but non-existent relations and realities (*umûrun 'adamiyah*). There is only the unique determination of the Essence, which is the Eminent in Itself, without relation to whatsoever it may be. And in this respect there is no relative eminence; but since the aspects of the One, contain a hierarchy amongst themselves, relative eminence is to be found implied in the unique determination (of the Being) by virtue of its multiple aspects. For this reason we say of the relative that it is Him (that is to say God) and it is not Him, and that thou are thee and not thee.

Abu Sa'îd al-Kharrâz, who is himself one of the multiple aspects of God and one of His tongues, says that God can only be known[2] by the synthesis of antinomic affirmations; for He is the First and the Last, the Exterior and the Interior; He is the essence of that which is manifested, and the essence of that which remains hidden after His manifestation. There is nobody other than He who can see Him, and nobody from whom He can hide Himself; It is He who manifests Himself to Himself, and it is He who hides Himself from Himself. It is He who calls Himself Abu Sa'îd al Kharrâz and by other names of ephemeral beings. The Interior says 'No' when the Exterior says 'Me'; and the Exterior says 'no' when the Interior says 'Me'. It follows in the same way for all antinomy; yet, there is only one who speaks, and He is Himself His own listener.

Thus, the realities are mingled : unity produces numbers according to their known series; and the numbers in their turn subdivide the unity. The number is not manifested without it being counted; and that which is subject to the number requires on one hand non-existence and on the other hand existence; for a thing may be absent on the sensible plane and existent in an intelligible manner. There is necessarily polarity of the number and of that which is subject to the number; and there is necessarily a production of the numbers from the unity onward, although each number represents a unique idea. Each number, in fact, on this side of the tenth, as well as beyond, until infinity, is in itself unique; its essential reality (*haqîqah*) is not conceivable quantitatively, by addition of unities; the binary for example, is a unique idea, so is the ternary, and thus for all the unlimited series of numbers; now, if each number represents a unique truth, no one of them can essentially understand the others, but the addition takes them

[2] Or 'defined'.

all by their order and affirms them all by virtue of this order, which comprises twenty degrees (units and tens) which combine themselves. Thus thou dost not cease to affirm this even though thou deniest 'a priori' (that is to say that thou affirmest continually the successive composition of the series of numbers, at the same time starting with the unique and indivisible idea that each number contains). He who understands that which we have been saying about the numbers, and that their negation is at the same time their affirmation knows that God, who is transcendent in the sense of *tanzîh* is (also) the 'comparable' creature in the sense of *tashbîh* – although the creature be distinct from the Creator.

Reality is the Creator created;[3] – or else the Reality is a creative creature.[4] All that is but the expression of a single essence – no, it is at the same time the Unique Essence (*al 'ayn*) and the multiple essences (*al a'yân*). Consider, then, that which thou seest!

(Isaac said to his father Abraham, who was preparing to sacrifice him) 'O my father, do that which thou hast been ordered'. Now, the child is (symbolically) the essence of his generator. When Abraham saw in his (inspired) dream that he was sacrificing his son, he saw himself in reality sacrificing himself. And when he redeemed his son by the sacrifice of the ram, he saw the reality which was manifested in the human form, manifest itself under the aspect of the ram. So it is thus, then, that the essence of the generator manifests itself in the form of the child, or more exactly, in relation to the child.

'(It is He who hath created you of one soul), and who from him created his wife.' (Koran, IV, I.) In other terms, Adam married his own soul; from him are descended both his companion and his child. It is thus that the (Divine) Order is unique in the multiplicity.

It is the same of Nature (*at-tabî 'ah*) and of that which proceeds from it.[5] Nature never diminishes because of its productions nor augments because of their re-absorption. That which it produces is none other than itself though it may not be, as such, identical to its productions in varied forms. This, for example, is cold and dry, and that hot and dry;[6] they are therefore homogeneous by dryness, but

---

[3] That is to say the Creator immanent to the creature.

[4] God manifesting Himself on account of the creature.

[5] Production which is inversely analogous of the manifestations of the essence.

[6] Nature has four fundamental determinations which express themselves in sensible order by, heat, cold, dryness, and humidity, qualities which one could call 'agents' of all the natural changes.

distinct by another quality. It is the common quality which is the Nature – or rather : the primordial determination (of all these qualities). The world of nature consists in (varied) forms (reflecting themselves) in a unique mirror; – or better : it is a single form (reflecting itself) in diverse mirrors.

It is thus that there is only perplexity (*hayrah*) because of contradictory perspectives. But he who understands what we have said does not fall into perplexity, even when he passes from one state of knowledge to another; for (the changing of perspective) arises only from the inherent condition of the 'place', (*mahal*, signifying the spiritual halt the receptive interior state); and the 'place' (in this sense) is only an immediate determination of the essence (*al-'ayn ath-thâbitah*) (of the being who contemplates God). It is by virtue of this (that is to say by virtue of this determination) that God differentiates Himself in the 'theatre' of His revelation, so that He assumes in turn diverse conditions; that which determines Him (apparently) is but the essential determination in which He reveals Himself. Nothing else exists. In one respect, God is creature – so, interpret ! – And He is not creature in another respect – so, remember !

As for the Eminent in Himself, He is the one who possesses the perfection (or the infinity : *al-kamâl*) in which are 'drowned' all the existential realities as well as all the non-existent relations (in themselves), in the sense that He is not without any of these 'attributes', whether the attribute be positive, logically or morally, or whether it be negative, according to custom, reason or moral. Now, this infinity belongs only to He who is designated by the name Allah (which is the Name of the Essence) exclusively; as for he who is designated by another name, it is either one of His 'planes of revelation' (*majlâ*) or a 'form' which is inherent to Him : if it is a 'place of revelation' it contains a hierarchical degree, in the same way that there is a distinction in that which is revealed and that in which He is revealed; on the other hand, if it is a question of a 'form' (in the sense of synthesis of the Qualities, contained) in God, this 'form' will be the immediate expression of the infinite; since it is essentially identical to that which is revealed in it.[7] All that which belongs to Allah, belongs then, equally to this (qualitative) 'form'. However, one does not say of this 'form' that it is He; but neither does one say it is other than He.

---

[7] So that all hierarchical distinction arises, from this point of view, from the receptive substance (*al-qâbil*).

It is to that, that the Imam Abu-l-Qâsim ibn Fâsi alluded in his book 'The removal of the Sandals', (of Moses before the burning bush), saying 'Truly, each Divine Name is qualified by all the Divine Names'. It is truly so; each Name, in fact, affirms the essences at the same time as the Essence, following its significance; in so far as it demonstrates the Essence, all the other Names are implied in it, and in so far as it affirms a particular significance, it distinguishes itself from the others like 'the Creator' distinguishes itself from 'He who gives the form' and so on. The Name, then, is on one hand essentially identical with the Named, and on the other hand, distinct from Him by its particular significance.

Of the Wisdom of Being Lost in Love
(al-hikmat al-muhaymiyah)
in the Word of Abraham

ABRAHAM is called (in the Koran) the 'Intimate Friend' (of God; *khalîl Allâh*)[1] because he 'penetrated' and assimilated the Qualities of the Divine Essence, like the colour which penetrates a coloured object, in such a manner that the accident is confused with the substance, and not like something spread out which fills a given space; or again, his name signifies that God (*al-haqq*) has penetrated essentially the form of Abraham. Each of these two affirmations is right, for each points to a certain aspect (of the state it concerns) without these two aspects cumulating.

Dost thou not see that God manifests Himself in the qualities of ephemeral beings, as He affirms, moreover, Himself (in the Divine Words)[2] that He manifests even in the qualities of imperfection and in the qualities deserving blame (or are such when they are related to man, like jealousy or anger, for example)? On the other hand, the creature manifests himself with the Divine Qualities, attributing to himself these from the first to the last; they really belong to the creature; in the same way as the qualities of the ephemeral beings belong really to God. 'The praise is to God';[3] that is to say that definitely all glory, of all that praises and of all that is praised, comes back to God alone. 'To God returns all reality' (*amr*);[4] this word includes the blameworthy as well as the praiseworthy; and there exists only the one and the other.[5]

---

[1] The word *khalîl* refers to the idea of penetration.

[2] The commentator an-Nâbulusî cites as an example the word, transmitted as *hadîth qudsî* ('Divine Word'): 'I have been hungry, and thou hast not nourished me; I have been ill, and thou hast not taken care of me'.

[3] Koran I, 2.

[4] Koran XI, 123.

[5] Al-Quashânî explains that evil is but a relative privation of the Being, that is, from good, evil having no existence in itself. Saint Dennis Areopagite had

When one thing is penetrated by something else, the first is contained by the second; for the penetrating hides itself in the penetrated,
so that the latter is apparent and the former, the interior, is latent;
the penetrating is also like the food of the penetrated, in the manner
that water spreads itself in wool and makes it heavier and more
voluminous. If it is the Divinity that appears, and the creature is found
hidden there, this latter is assimilated into all the Names of God, into
His hearing, into His seeing, into all His attributes and His modes of
knowledge; in return, if it is the creature who is apparent and the
Divinity is immanent to him and is found hidden within, God is the
hearing of the created being, his sight, his hand, his foot and all his
faculties, as is said in this Divine Word surely transmitted ('My servant
cannot approach Me with something which would please Me more
than that which I have imposed upon him. And My servant approaches Me without ceasing by his surrogative works until I love him;
and when I love him, I am the hearing by which he hears, the sight
by which he sees, the hand with which he takes and the foot with
which he walks'.)

If the Essence was exempt from these (universal) relations (which
are the Divine Names and Qualities) It would not be Divinity (*ilâh*;
that is to say, It would not be Creator). Now, these relations become
actualized by virtue of our own determinations (which are in some
ways the objects of it or the passive contents) so that we render the
Divinity such by our dependence on Him. God is not, then, known as
such (that is to say as Creator and Lord) before we are known; which
corresponds to the word of the Prophet: 'he who knows himself (or:
knows his soul), – knows his Lord'; and the Prophet was certainly he
who knew best the creatures through God. For certain sages, and
amongst them Abu-Hâmid (*al-Ghazzâlî*) claimed that God can be
known disregarding the world; but that is false.[6] Certainly, the eternal
Essence knows Itself; but it is not known as Divinity before one knows
that which depends on It, and which is thus the symbol which proves
It. Then only, in the second state of knowledge, thou wilt have the
intuition that God Himself is the symbol of Himself and of His Divine

---

already exposed the same truth. As a particularly striking example, al-Qashânî
mentions the bad passion of the lover, which is blameworthy, not in its essence,
which is love, but accidentally, that is to say in so far as it contradicts its own
essence; integral love.

[6] It is a question of a difference of perspectives, so an extrinsic incompatibility
of points of view, for the wise ones are not mistaken.

Nature, that the world is but His own revelation in the forms of un-alterable essences, which do not exist in any fashion outside Him, and that He assumes diverse forms and modes following the realities which are implied by the essences, and according to their states. But we receive this intuition only after having realized through God that we depend on a Divinity. After (these two consecutive states of conscious-ness) there opens yet a last intuition, according to which our forms appear to thee in God, so that beings manifest themselves, the one and the other in God, recognizing one another and distinguishing one from another. Certain of us know of this reciprocal knowledge in God, and others are ignorant of the Divine Presence in which is revealed this knowledge of ourselves. May God protect me from ignorance!

From the one as from the other of these two intuitions (succeeding from the first), it follows that God judges us only by ourselves, or more exactly, it is we ourselves who judge ourselves, but through Him. And it is for that, that He says in the Koran 'to God is the decisive argu-ment' (VI, 150) against the illusioned ones when they will say to God 'Why hast thou done with us this or that', (thinking of) that which was contrary to their interests; 'then a leg will be revealed to them',[7] which means precisely the reality which is revealed to those who know God from this life. And they will see that it is not God who did to them that which they claimed that He did but that it came from themselves; for He simply makes them know what they are in them-selves (in their permanent possibilities). From thence, their argument will dissolve, and there will exist only the 'decisive argument of God'.

Maybe thou wilt say: what then is the sense of the Divine Word 'If He had wanted, He would have guided all of you'?[8] To which we will reply: the proposition 'laww' (which is translated by 'if', in the sentence 'if He had wanted etc . . .') has the sense of the imaginary abolition of an obstacle (If He had not wanted at all) so, He wanted only that which really happened. According to the logical definition, a possibility is that which can or cannot actually happen; but in reality the effective solution of this purely rational alternative is already found implied in that which is this possibility in its state of principial immutability. As for the expression '. . . He would have guided you all . . .' it means: He would have shown to all (your illusion); only, it does not come into

---

[7] Arabic expression which means that the reality of a thing is revealed naked. (Koran LXVIII, 41.)
[8] Koran LXVIII, 41.

the possibility of every being in this world that God opens the eye of their intuitive intelligence so that he sees the reality such as it is; there are those who know and those who do not. So, God did not want to guide them all, and did not guide them all, and He would not want to do so; and even if He wanted – but how then could He want something which has not taken place?

The Divine Will is one, in its relationship (with its objects).[9] As an essential relation it depends on the knowledge (just as man conceives first that which he wants); and knowledge depends on its object; now, this object is thee and thy states. It is not the knowledge which has an effect on that which is known, but this latter which acts on the knowledge, in the sense that it communicates itself to it alone, according to that which is in its own essence.[10]

As for the Divine discourse (revealed in the Koran and in other sacred books, where God manifests Himself as a Person), it has been revealed in conformity with the understanding of those to whom it is addressed and in conformity with reason, and not according to the ways of intuition. It is for that, moreover, that there are many believers and few who know intuitively. But 'each of us has our determined position'[11] which means : such as thou art in thy permanent state (that

---

[9] Its apparent diversity proceeds from the possibilities that it embraces.

[10] In his book 'Of Universal Man', the sufi, Abd al-Karîm al-Jîlî, writes on this subject: '. . . it is not exact to say that the objects of knowledge affirm themselves in this by themselves, because that would result in God drawing from something other than Himself. The Imâm Muhyi-d-din Ibn 'Arabi has expressed himself in a defective manner in saying that objects of Divine Knowledge communicate by themselves to this. We will excuse him and will not say that that is all that he knew. As for us, we have found that God knows all in principle, without His Knowledge resulting from the nature of His objects as such; only, these objects imply, as such, that which God already knows of them principially, and in this second respect they affirm their own essences in Him . . .' (chapter on Knowledge) – The divergence of the two points of view may be explained thus: for Ibn 'Arabi, the objects of the Divine Knowledge are the 'immutable essences' (al-a'yân ath-thâbitah) which do not have a proper existence, but which are but inherent possibilities in the infinite Essence. The ambiguity, in the expression of Ibn 'Arabi, comes, then, from the fact that he speaks of these essences as distinct realities, and in this sense Jîlî is right to contradict him. But the intellectual 'vision' of Ibn 'Arabi contains the following synthesis: Divine Knowledge draws from the essential possibilities, which are nothing else but God; it 'conceives' at the same time these essences as such and all that they imply in so far as relative developments, and, because of that it is absolute in its identification with the Absolute, and it appears as relative in its identification with the relative.

[11] Koran XXXVII, 164.

is to say as pure possibility) thou wilt manifest thyself in thy (relative) existence always supposing that thou dost exist: but in return, if existence is attributable to God only, and not to thee, then it is, without doubt, thee who will judge thyself (or thou who wilt determine) in Divine Existence (because thou art then entirely determination and nothing more); but if one admits it is thou who art the existing (and that thou art not only pure determination), the judgement again belongs to thee (by virtue of that which thou art), even if the Judge is God. From God comes only the effusion of the Being on thee (who art only pure possibility); whereas thine own judgement (or thy determination) comes from thee.

Then, praise only thyself, and blame only thyself. To God is due only the praises for His effusion of the Being (or of the Existence) for that comes from Him alone, and not from thee (for thou art non-existent as such). From then on thou art His nourishment because thou lendest to Him thy conditions, and He is thy nourishment by the Existence (al-wujûd) that He communicated to you, so that He is determined by that which determines thee. The Order (al-amr) goes from Him to thee and from thee to Him, although thou art the 'obligated one' (by the revealed Law) and He is not the 'obligated one' (by His Own Law); and moreover, He imposed on thee (the Order) only because thou asked Him, by thine own state and by that which thou art.

> He praises me, and I praise Him;
> He serves me, and I serve Him;
> By my existence I affirm Him;
> And by my determination I deny Him;
> It is He who knows me, when I deny Him;
> Then I discover Him and contemplate Him.
> Where then is His independence, when I glorify Him and help
>   Him?[12]
> In the same way, as soon as God manifests me,
> I lend Him science and manifest Him,
> It is that which the Divine Message teaches us.
> And it is in me that His Will is accomplished.

[12] It is still a question of God (al-haqq) in His 'personal' aspect, correlative to the creation, and not of the Absolute Essence, in the face of which the creature is nothing.

From the time that Abraham had reached the degree of knowledge by reason of which he was called the 'Intimate Friend' (of God) he made of hospitality a sacred custom;[13] so Ibn Massara[14] associates him (in his cosmological function) to Michael, the angel who provides the (physical and spiritual) nourishment (of beings).[15] For nourishment penetrates the entire body of he whom it nourishes, until it be assimilated by the smallest parts of the body. Of course, there are no parts in the Divinity (to which applies the symbol of the penetrated body); that which is penetrated, in this case are the Divine 'Stations' (*maqâmât*) which one calls the Names[16] and through which the Divine Essence manifests Itself.

> We are His as evidence establishes,
> And we are our own;
> He is only Himself through my existence,
> So that we are His as we are by ourselves.
> I have two aspects: He and me;
> And He is not His Me in me,
> But He finds there His place of manifestation.
> We are then for Him, like receptacles.

God tells the truth and guides one on the right path.[17]

---

[13] His hospitality towards the three Angels of the Lord being the model of all hospitality.

[14] Andalusian Sufi who taught cosmology.

[15] The Sufi cosmology is attached to 'angelology' in the same way that the natural world is attached to the spiritual world.

[16] Since the Divine Names or the Qualities contain necessarily a hierarchical order, one can also call them the 'degrees' or the 'stations' of the principial manifestation of God.

[17] That which Ibn 'Arabi teaches in this chapter 'Meister' Eckhart expresses in these words: 'In the principle, I was, I thought of myself as myself, I myself wanted to produce this man that I am, I am my own cause from my essence which is eternal, as according to my apparition in time. That which I have been in eternity, I am now, and will remain always, whereas that which I am in time will pass and will be destroyed with time itself. In the act of my eternal birth, all things have been begotten with me, and I have become the cause of myself and all the rest, and if I wanted it, I would not yet be either myself nor everything else; if I was not, God would not be' (cf. Emmanuel Aegerter: *Le Mysticisme*. Paris 1952, p. 78).

Of the Wisdom of the Truth
(al-hikmat al-naqqiyah)
in the Word of Isaac

The redemption of a prophet (Isaac having been a prophet) by the
    sacrifice of an animal as an offering:
How then are the bleating of sheep and the word of man of equal
    value?
God the Magnificent (saying in the Koran: 'and we have redeemed
    him by a great sacrifice') magnified the ram,
Helping it by us or helping us by it,[1] – I do not see by virtue of what
    balance ₈ ₌ .'[2]
The camel and the bovine are no doubt bigger bodily,
And yet, they gave their rank to a ram sacrificed as an offering.
How can I know how a ram replaced
By its little body the representant of the Merciful on earth?
But dost thou not see that the commandment (to sacrifice the ram in
    the place of Isaac) implies a logical order,
Assuring the gain and compensating the loss?[3]
For there is not one (earthly) creature superior to the mineral,
Then to vegetable, according to its degree and its ranks;

[1] In replacing the human victim, the sacrificed animal 'helps' man in his
reconciliation with Heaven. On the other hand, he who sacrifices, benefits the
animal in making it participate in the sacerdotal function of man, mediator
between 'Heaven' and 'Earth'. As in Judaism, Islam perpetuates ritually the
sacrifice of Abraham by the sacrifice of a ram. For Christians, the sacrifice of
Abraham represents the sacrifice of Christ, in his turn perpetuated by the
Eucharistic rite.

[2] The object to be sacrificed cannot be replaced except by that which contains
it essentially.

[3] If man is superior to animal by his active participation in the Intelligence,
animal is on its side superior to man by its primordial nature, that is to say by
its fidelity to its cosmic norm; it is in this sense that a noble animal reveals an
interior and supra-rational aspect of even the essence of man, and it is that which
constitutes the 'logical order' of sacrifice, assuring the gain for man and 'compensating the loss' for the animal.

And it is after the plant that the animal[4] comes into this hierarchy;

Each one (of the beings of these three reigns) knows his Creator by
    direct intuition (*kashf*) and by evident signs;[5]

Whereas man is conditioned (in his knowledge of God) by reason,
    thought, and the dogma of his belief.

It is that which Sahl (al Tostarî) affirmed, and he who knows reality,[6]
    as do we,

For all – we and you – we are in the station of contemplative virtue
    (*al-ihsân*).

Each of us who contemplates the reality which I have contemplated,

Will say the same, in secret and openly.

So do not turn towards those who contradict us,

And do not sow grain in the land of the blind!

For it is they who are the deaf and the dumb of whom spake – for our
    ears –

He who was exempt from sin (the Prophet) in the Koran.

Know – may God help us, thou and us – that Abraham, the friend
of God, said to his son; 'In truth, I have seen in a (prophetic) dream
that I was sacrificing thee'.[7] Now, the dream is drawn from the Imaginative Presence (*hadarat al-khayâl*, that is to say from the Divine
Presence in subtle forms or images); however, Abraham did not transpose his dream – (from the symbol to the reality symbolized as one is
urged to do for that which manifests itself in this state); it was a ram

---

[4] This affirmation appears to contradict the doctrine revealed, according to
which man is the representative of God on earth, all other earthly beings in
submission to him. However, if it is thus according to a certain perspective,
meaning that which envisages the spiritual possibilities of beings, the inverse
order is equally real, according to a certain other point of view, for the 'substantial' perfection of beings is in a way in opposition to their essential virtues; the
world – says Ibn 'Arabi in the chapter on Seth – is like a mirror, 'where the
realities invert themselves and become ambiguous'. It is by virtue of this law of
inversion that the diamond, for example, is the most perfect image of the Spirit
or Intellect, – although the latter be pure act and the mineral be that which is
the most passive in our world. The superiority of man over other earthly beings
– who were created before him, – is of a relatively 'interior' nature, whereas the
superiority of animal over man, or of the plant over the animal, or of the
mineral over the plant, consists in a greater 'exteriorisation' of essential perfections. See on this subject: Frithjof Schuon '*De l'Unité transcendante des
Religions*' p. 68 sqq.

[5] That is to say by a contemplation in a way natural, which is confused with
the essential 'form' of the species.

[6] The Sufi Abu Yazîd al-Bastâmi.

[7] Koran XXXVII, 102.

which appeared in the dream in the form of Abraham's son, and Abraham believed in this dream; but God redeemed the child from the illusion (*wahm*) of Abraham by the 'great sacrifice' (of the ram), which was the Divine transposition of which Abraham had not been conscious.[8]

For the formal revelation in the Imaginative Presence can only be understood with the help of another science which allows one to discern that which God wants to give us to understand by a determined form. – Dost thou remember how the messenger of God – May Benediction and Peace be on him! – said to Abu Bakr, when the latter interpreted a certain dream: 'Thou hast guessed partly right, but thou hast missed the meaning of another part'? Then Abu Bakr asked the Prophet to make known to him what he had said right and in what he was mistaken; but the Prophet did not answer him.[9]

[8] In the chapter on Enoch, Ibn 'Arabi indicates another aspect of this sacrifice, of an even more 'interior' order; the child is a symbol of the soul – or of the interior reality – of his begetter; thence, the sacrifice of the child itself, signifies the sacrifice of oneself; thus the ram is the symbol of the soul of Abraham. The latter sees his soul on one hand, in his interior vision, in the form of his son; it appeared to him on the other hand, in the exterior world, in the form of a ram. It is necessary here to specify that the Koran speaks of a vision (*rûyâ*) or of a prophetic dream which had determined Abraham to sacrifice his son.
The episode commented on shows the double refraction of eternal realities in the world of forms, which is distinguished in a 'subjective' domain, and an 'objective' domain, both englobed in the cosmic 'imagination' (*al-khayâl*); the apparition of the soul in the form of the son is revealed from a 'subjective' projection, whereas the transposition of the child to the ram springs from the complementality of the microcosm and the macrocosm: in this latter the sacrificial animal occupies the rank which symbolically reverts to 'son of man'.

[9] The episode in question is the following: 'a man came to the Prophet and said to him: last night I saw in a dream a cloud out of which fell fat and honey. And I saw people who gathered it up with their hands; some received a lot, and some a little. And I saw a rope which came down from the sky to the earth; thou didst seize it and wert drawn up to the sky; a man seized it after thee and also became drawn up; then another seized it and again was elevated; then another seized it and fell; then he tried again and was drawn up. – Then Abu Bakr said: O messenger of God, by my father, by thee and by God, if thou dost permit me I will interpret it. The messenger of God said: interpret it. Abu Bakr said: As for the cloud, it is the cloud of Islâm; as for the downfall of fat and honey, that signifies the gentleness and unction of the Koran, of which people gather more or less. The rope which descends from the sky to the earth is the truth which thou dost hold; thou dost seize it and God elevates thee by it; then a man seizes it after thee and is drawn up; then another man seizes it and is drawn up, then another seizes it and falls back; then he tries again and is likewise drawn up. Tell me now, O messenger of God, by my father, have I said truly or falsely? The messenger of

God said to Abraham, when He called him : 'In truth, O Abraham, thou hast believed in the vision!',[10] which does not mean that Abraham, believing that he must sacrifice his son, was faithful to the Divine inspiration; for he took his vision word for word, whereas every dream requires a transposition or interpretation. That is why Joseph's master in Egypt said : '. . . if you know how to interpret dreams . . .'[11] to interpret means to transpose the perceived form to another reality; (in the case mentioned) the cows signified the years which were fertile or meagre. If God praised Abraham for having been faithful to his vision, it would have been necessary for him really to kill his son, for he had believed the sacrifice of his son was meant, whereas it symbolised, from the Divine point of view, the 'great sacrifice' (of the ram).[12] The child was, then, redeemed in Abraham's mind only, not in reality and from the Divine point of view.

There is then, an analogy between the corporal form of the ram and the imaginary form of Abraham's son. If Abraham had seen a ram in his dream he would have interpreted it as signifying his son or something else. God next said to Abraham : 'In truth, this is the test (rendered) evident',[13] which means that God put his knowledge to the test, proving whether or not he knew what the perspective belonging to the imaginative vision required as interpretation.[14]

God replied: thou hast divined right in part and thou hast missed the meaning in another part. He said: By God, oh messenger of God, tell me where I missed the meaning. He replied: do not oblige me!' – An Nâbulusî, who tells this story according to Muslim, remarks that the vision of the three men who seized the rope after the Prophet was probably concerning the three Caliphs of which the first was Abu Bakr himself and the third Othman, against whom other Muslims rose up, who was assassinated by the rebels and recognised as a saint after his death.

[10] Koran XXXVII, 105.

[11] Koran XII, 42.

[12] Thus the vision of Abraham indicated the ritual sacrifice of the ram, without which, moreover, it would not have been prophetic. Let us add that it was a question of a 'great sacrifice' because henceforth the ritual sacrifice was to replace that of human victims. See on this subject Frithjof Schuon: 'L'Œil du Coeur', chap: 'Du Sacrifice'.

[13] Koran XXXVII, 106.

[14] According to the common interpretation of the sacred history which is in question, God tested Abraham in his fidelity, not in his knowledge, and this sense seems to impose itself as the most religious; however, all Divine 'tests' return, eventually, to a limitation of the knowledge of he who is subjected to it; this limitation may be substantial, as amongst most mortals, or accidental at the same time as providential, as happens with the Prophets; the test results

For Abraham knew quite well that the cosmic state of imagination required an interpretation, but he did not take it into account, not considering the condition inherent to the state (of the matter in question); he believed in the vision just as it presented itself,[15] just as Taqî ibn Mukhallad, the transmitter of oral traditions, who learnt by a way which was certain that the Prophet had said : 'Whoever sees me in a dream sees me as if in a state of wakefulness, for Satan cannot assume my form'; now, Taqî ibn Mukhallad saw in a dream the Prophet who gave him a bowl of milk to drink; he believed in the vision, but forced himself to vomit, (to verify it), upon which he threw up enough milk to fill a bowl. If he had interpreted his dream, he would have known that the milk means knowledge; (but acting in such a way) he frustrated himself of a great knowledge, equal to what he drank. Dost thou not see how the Messenger of God – Benediction and Peace be on him ! – received in a dream a basin of milk and he told how he drank it, 'until satiety came out of my nails; and it is thus that it was given to me that which I bestowed on Omar'. It was said to him 'And for what dost thou take it (this milk), O Messenger of God?' He answered : 'For knowledge.' So he did not simply take it for milk, knowing that the state in which the vision took place required a transposition.

Now, one knows that the corporal form of the Prophet – May God Bless him and give him Peace ! – is buried at Medina, and that his spiritual form – the same as his subtle reality – has never been seen by

---

always in an apparent contradiction of Divine promises or more generally of Divine revelations; he who is situated intellectually above the relative plane where these contradictions appear, is not subjected to them. On the other hand, the object of the test is precisely to go beyond the domain of 'imaginary' contrasts. In the case of Abraham, the apparent order to sacrifice his son contradicted the promise of posterity that God had made him before the birth of his son. From another point of view, the resignation of Abraham to the sacrifice of his posterity was the intrinsic condition for the 'sacralisation' of the latter. From the Christian point of view, one would say that Abraham's intentional sacrifice was preparing the coming of Christ. One may thus observe that faith in Divine promises, in spite of their apparent obscurity, replaces provisionally the knowledge of that which they imply, and draws them finally to the explanation.

[15] For there are certain appearances in the world of dreams that one must take 'literally', without applying to them the law of inverse analogy, as will be seen by what follows. These apparitions are in a way sovereignly symbolic, and not accidentally submitted to the conditions of the imaginative state; such is the case, for Islâm, of the apparitions of the Prophet.

anyone; since we cannot even see our own spiritual form, it is the same for all spirits. But the spirit of the Prophet assumes, when he appears in somebody's dream, the form of his body just as he was before death, without anything missing,[16] so that he is really Muhammed – Peace be on him! – appearing through his spirit in a subtle body (jasad) resembling his buried body, for Satan cannot assume the subtle form of the Prophet, God thus protecting those who see him. Let those who see the Prophet in this form, then, receive the orders that the Prophet will be able to give him, or the news that he will be able to communicate to them, just as one received the teachings of the Prophet during his lifetime, conforming to the immediate sense, figuratively or implicitly put into words, or whatever the form of expression. But if he gives him something (in a dream), it will be this thing that will be subject to the transposition, unless the thing manifests itself in the waking state just as it was in the dream, for in this case there is no transposition to be made with regard to it. It was this aspect of the vision that Abraham, the Friend of God, put his trust, in the same way as Taqî ibn Mukhallad.

Since the vision (in dreams) requires two aspects (a direct aspect and an aspect subject to interpretation), and God taught us what should be our attitude, by what He did with Abraham and by what He said to him – (this teaching) springing precisely from the prophetic function (of Abraham) – we know that on seeing God – May He be Exalted! – in a form that reason refutes (as being God, for it is reason that infers transcendence), we must interpret this form as being conditioned Divinity, be it by the state of he who sees Him, be it by the 'cosmic place' (al-makân) where it is seen, or again by the two things at once. On the other hand, if reason does not refute it, we take it directly for that which it is, like when we see God on the other side . . . To the Unique, the Clement, (ar-rahmân) belongs, in each state of

[16] Since the Prophet himself is the symbol 'par excellence', his appearance in the dream cannot be subject to the refraction which would inverse the form. And we would say, that in the Christian world the appearances of the Virgin have a character equally direct, whereas those of Christ do not necessarily come under this law, because Christ is identified for the Christian to the Divinity which manifests Itself under all possible aspects. The great masters of the 'Hesychast' for example, have never failed to warn against satanic apparitions imitating the image of Christ; it goes without saying that such imitations will always carry some sign of their falseness. The person of the Prophet – like that of the Virgin – contains a quality of 'perfect servitude' ('ubûdiyah) which Satan would not be able to imitate.

existence, all forms hidden or manifested. If thou sayest: this is God! thou sayest the truth; but when thou affirmest something else, it is then that thou dost interpret. His principle (of manifestation) does not change from one state of existence to the other; but He produces the Truth to His creatures. When He reveals Himself to the eyes, the reason refutes Him by insistent proofs; on the other hand, He is accepted in His intellectual revelation, and in that which one calls imagination (khayâl); but the true (vision) is the direct 'vision'. Abu Yazîd (al-Bastâmî) says of this last spiritual station: 'even if the Divine Throne and all that it contains was contained one hundred million times in one of the corners of the heart of the believer (of God) he would not feel it' – It is there the magnitude of Abu Yazîd in the world of 'corporal' forms (for the Throne is here symbolically conceived as an extended form); but as for me, I say: even if the limitlessness of all that exists could be conceived as being limited and it was contained, with the essence (al-'ayn) that unites it, in one of the corners of the heart of a believer (in God), he would not be conscious of it; for it is said that the heart contains God – May He be Exalted! – and still does not reach satiety; and if it was full it would be saturated. – And this Abu Yazîd said equally.[17]

We have already alluded to this spiritual station, saying: 'O Thou, Who createth everything in Thyself; Thou englobeth all that Thou createth; now, Thou createth that whose existence has no end in Thee, so that Thou art the Narrow, the Vast! If that which God created was in my heart, His resplendent dawn would not shine therein; but, that which contains God excludes no creature; how then can that be, O Thou who hearest?'

All that man creates by conjecture (wahm), in his imaginative faculty, is that which has no existence outside it. That is something common (to all). But he who knows (God) creates by his spiritual will (al-himmah) that which acquires an existence outside the seat of this faculty.[18] However, the spiritual will, will not cease to conserve in

[17] Sahl-al-Tostarî having sent him the message: 'here is a man who drank a drink which leaves him for ever refreshed', Abu Yazîd replied: 'here is a man who has drunk all existences, but whose mouth is dry and burns with thirst'.

[18] That is to say that the form thus created has not only a subjective reality, even though it is of a subtle nature. For this 'creation', the imaginative faculty (al-khayâl) will play only the role of the passive substance; the qualitative form of the 'creature' will be determined by al-himmah, that is to say the 'spiritual will' or 'force of spiritual decision' which is not of purely individual

existence that which it has created, without it being impaired by this conservation; each time that the believer forgets to maintain thus in existence that which he created by his spiritual will, his creature will cease to exist; unless the believer has realized all the (Divine) Presences and does not forget one; certainly, his conscience will be drawn necessarily, towards one of the Presences (and not to all at once, for he would then cease to exist himself); but if the believer has created by his spiritual will that which he has created, and he possesses that total knowledge (englobing in principle all the Divine Presences), his creature will manifest his 'form' (meaning the 'form' of the believer) in each of the Presences, so that the (analogous) 'forms' (appearing in the different states) will maintain each other in existence;[19] if the believer becomes unconscious of any of the Presences or of many Presences – at the same time upholding, in the (Divine) Presence that he continues to contemplate, the existence of the 'form' that he has created all the (analogous) 'forms' will be conserved by the maintenance of this particular 'form' in the Presence of which he remains conscious. – For consciousness is never total, neither in ordinary men, nor in the elite. – By this, I have just exposed a secret, the nature of which the initiates have

---

impulsion, but corresponds to the ray of Divine activity in man. One will remark the antinomy between the conjecture (al-wahm, a word which also means opinion and suspicion) and the spiritual will (al-himmah).

[19] From the fact that this 'creature' is the object of an incessant spiritual concentration, it cannot be anything else but the symbol of the Essence. It is therefore necessary to relate this passage to that in which Ibn 'Arabi says elsewhere, in the chapter on Muhammed, of the impossibility of 'contemplating' the Essence without support. – 'Abd al Karîm-al-Jîlî wrote in his book Al-Insân al-kâmil ('Of Universal Man'): 'If the imagination fashions some form in the mental state, this imaginary form is created; but, in every creature the Creator is present; on the other hand, this imagination is in thee, so that thou art, in relation to it, like God (al-haqq). The fashioning of (mental) forms returns necessarily to thee, but in God, and God (al-haqq) is present there'. (Chapter on ar-rahmâniyah). The Divine Presence in the mental forms, as 'Abd al-Karîm al-Jîlî considers it, is purely principial; but if the mental form corresponds to a revealed symbol, the Presence will be virtually there, and if the integral act of man, al-himmah, coincided with the symbol, the Divine Presence will be actual; it is this latter case which Ibn 'Arabi envisages. By its spiritual actualization, the symbol acquires a reality independent from the individual sphere of the contemplative, and since it implies really that which it expresses, it resumes all the modalities of the Divine Presence or all the states of the Being; on the other hand, as the contemplative himself is identified by his integral act, to this symbolic form, this 'unfolds' him in turn in all the states of the Being. See also on this subject: Frithjof Schuon, 'L'Oeil du Coeur' chap. 'Microcosme et Symbole'.

always jealously hidden, for it contains a refutation of their pretention of identification with God; for God – May He be Exalted! – is never unconscious of anything, whereas the servant is necessarily unconscious of one thing in favour of another; but, in so much as the servant himself maintains in existence that which he has created, he can say: I am God; only, he does not maintain it in the sense of the Divine conservation; we have just explained the difference. In so much as the servant remains conscious of one of the 'forms' in a particular presence, he distinguishes himself from God; he distinguishes himself necessarily, although all the (analogous) 'forms' be maintained in existence by the maintenance of a single one amongst those appearing in the Presence of which the believer remains conscious – which is conservation by implicit guarantee; – for the Divine conservation with regard to the created is not like this, but God conserves each 'form' in particular. This question which I have just exposed, nobody has mentioned in writing until now, neither I, nor others; the mention of it, then, is unique in its time, without precedent; be careful not to forget it!

Now, this (Divine) Presence of which thou remainest conscious at the same time as the 'form' which corresponds to it, is comparable to the Book where God writes everything: 'We have been negligent of nothing in this book'[20] – in such a way that it integrates at the same time that which is manifested and that which is not.[21] But nobody will understand that which we have just said except he who is himself Koran.[22] On the other hand he who 'fears' God will be gifted with discrimination (*al-furqan*)[23] (which distinguishes the Absolute from the conditional), according to the Divine Word ('Oh you who believe, if you fear God, He will endow you with discrimination') (VIII, 29). Now, this discrimination applies itself precisely to that which we were saying

[20] Koran VI, 38.

[21] That is to say that the 'real Presence' which has for support the form of a symbol, actualized by spiritual concentration, implies all reality in a global and indifferentiated manner.

[22] He who finds himself in a state of global knowledge. *Al-qu'rân*, literally: 'the reading' or the 'recitation', designates the unitative aspect of the revelation and, consequently, unitative knowledge in general, that is to say the knowledge of the essential unity of the non-created and the created.

[23] *Al furqân* 'the discrimination', designates the legislative aspect of the revelation and then the distinctive knowledge, or more exactly the discrimination of the non-created and the created. The unitative knowledge is reflected in love, whereas the discrimination has for psychic corollary, fear. In the spiritual way, these two aspects of knowledge must be balanced.

about the manner in which the servant distinguishes himself from the Lord. It is there the highest 'discrimination' that one can conceive.

> At one moment the servant will be the Lord (by union), without
> doubt,
> And at one moment the servant will be the servant (by discrimina-
> tion) certainly. If he is the servant, he is vast through God,
> And if he is the Lord, he is in a restricted life.

In so far as he is the servant, he sees his own essence, and his hopes start from him; but in so far as he is the Lord (by the extinction of his individuality in the pure light of the Intellect), he sees the whole cosmos, from the earth to the angels, who ask him, and he sees himself powerless to satisfy their demands by himself (in so far as he remains the servant in spite of the re-absorption of the Divine Light). It is for that reason that thou wilt see certain contemplatives weeping. So, then, be the servant (by thy manifest conscience, as well as being) Lord (by thine essential identification with God) and do not be (in thy distinctive conscience) Lord of thine own servant, so that thou dost not become prey of the fire (of the Divine Rigour); and that thou mayst not be delivered to the fusion.[24]

---

[24] All this passage refers to the spiritual economy ruled by the two aspects, unitative and discriminating, of Knowledge.

Extract from the Chapter:
Of the Sublime Wisdom *(al-hikmat al-'aliyah)* in the Word of Ismaël

KNOW that He who is called Allâh is one in the Essence and all by His names and that all conditioned being is only attached (as such) to God by his own Lord *(rabb)* exclusively; for it is impossible that the totality (of the Names or the Divine aspects) correspond to a particular being. For that which is of the Divine Unity *(al-ahadiyah)* none participate in it, for one cannot designate aspects to it; it is not subject to distinction. The Unity of God integrates the totality (of the Names or the Qualities) in the principial indifferentiation.

The 'happy one' *(as-sa'îd)* is he in whom 'the Lord is content';[1] now, there exists nobody with whom his own Lord is not content; for it is by him (that is to say this relative being) that his lordship exists, and every being then, is 'accepted' by his Lord and (in this respect) each one is 'content'. It is for this reason that Sahl al-Tostari said: 'the Divine, Lordship *(ar-rubûbiyah)* contains a secret, and this secret is Thyself' – he is addressing every individual –, 'if He could manifest Himself (that is to say, if He could be known through others), the Lordship would be abolished';[2] he says: 'if He could manifest himself . . .' because in fact He never manifests Himself, so that the Lordship will never be abolished. For no individual exists independently from his Lord (which is the 'polarisation' of the Divine Act towards him); on the other hand this individual exists perpetually (that is to say through all the precise existences, indefinitely – but not eternally) in such a way that the Lordship (which is based on him) equally exists perpetually.

He who is (in principle) accepted by his Lord is loved by Him; and all that the loved one does is equally loved; everything is, then, accept-

[1] Koran XIX, 55.
[2] The 'Lord' of such and such an individual is then no less than the 'person', according to the scholastic term 'persona', that is to say the essential reality of which the individual is the ephemeral expression.

ed by the Lord; for the individual would not know how to act unless
the action belonged to the Lord which acts in him. It is for this that
the individual (knowing his Lord) is 'appeased', confident that no
action will be attributed to him, and that he is happy that that which
appears in him is from the actions of his Lord[3] who, He, accepts these
actions, for every author is happy with his work, since he perfects his
work according to that which his nature demands; thus it is said in
the Koran : 'He who gives to everything his nature whom then He
guides';[4] that is to say : then He reveals that it is He who gave to
everything its nature, so that it would know how to be neither more
nor less (than that which it is).

'Ismaël was accepted by his Lord'[5] because he realized that which
we have just explained. Again, every being that exists is (in principle)
accepted by his Lord, without that implying necessarily that each one
is accepted by the Lord of the other, for the Lordship is only defined
with regard to each particular one, (because it is the 'personal' relationship of the individual towards God), so that it concerns God only
according to one of His aspects, which corresponds to the predispositions (isti 'dad) of the individual; that is, the 'Lord' of this particular
individual – no one (particular being) attaches itself (as such) to God
by virtue of His (supreme) Unity. It is because of this that the men of
God cannot receive the 'revelation' (tajallî) in the Unity (al-ahadiyah);
for if thou contemplatest Him through Himself, it is He who is contemplating Himself; – He does not then cease to be Himself contemplating Himself by Himself; and if thou contemplatest Him through
thyself, Unity ceases to be Unity, because of thee; if thou contemplatest Him through Him and through thee, Unity again ceases to be
that which it is, because the pronoun of the second person supposes
that there is something else there than only the contemplated; there
will be necessarily some relation, and following that a duality of the
contemplator and the one contemplated, from whence the cessation of
Unity, although there exists (in principle) only He who contemplates
Himself, for thou knowest well that neither the contemplating nor the
contemplated is 'other than He'.

Consequently it is not possible that the individual 'accepted by his

---

[3] Which is the same as saying that the beatitude of the soul consists in its
conscious conformity to its essence.
[4] Koran XX, 50.
[5] Koran XIX, 55.

Lord' be accepted (by God) absolutely,[6] unless all that he manifests comes from the accepting Lord, who acts through him.[7]

It is thus that Ismaël is distinguished from other individuals because it is said of him that he has been 'accepted by his Lord'. For it is the same for every 'peaceful' soul to which is addressed the (Koranic) word: 'Come back to thy Lord' (LXXXIX, 27 : 'O thou, peaceful soul : Come back to thy Lord, content, accepted; enter amongst My servants, and enter into My paradise'), that is to say : Come to the Lord who called you of old and that thou hast recognised amongst the totality (of the Divine Aspects) – 'content, accepted; enter amongst My servants' – adoring Me in this spiritual station; for among the servants who are spoken of here is whosoever has recognised his Lord, is satisfied with Him and does not turn towards the Lord of another servant,[8] at the same time recognising eminently the essential Unity (of all beings); – 'and enter My paradise (*jannah*)' – that is to say, in My veil (the word jannah, meaning 'garden' and 'paradise' implying the meaning of 'hiding'), this paradise being no other than thyself, for it is thee who veil Me by this human nature; I am known only by them as thou dost exist only by Me; who knows thee knows Me; although nobody (except Myself) knows Me (essentially), in the same way that thou too, thou art not known by anybody. Now, if thou enterest into His Paradise, thou enterest into thyself, and thou wilt know thyself by another knowledge different to that which made thee know thy Lord (in knowing thy soul) so that thou wilt possess two sorts of knowledge : thou wilt know God with respect to thee, and thou wilt know Him through thyself in so much as it is Him, not because thou dost exist.

[6] Since it exists only by virtue of a particular Divine 'Relation', which is its 'raison d'être' as an individual; so the human term of this relation is denied by other Divine 'relations', in the same way as the finite as such is denied by the infinite.

[7] So that it may all be integrated in his essential quality which cannot be in contradiction with the other Divine Qualities, for the Divine Qualities contradict each other only in their effects. Al Qashânî explains that the individual thus conforming to his Lord is thereby conforming to the Universal Lord and identified with the Perfect Man.

[8] Because the Divine Lordship supposes a unique personal relation which by definition is situated beyond all 'horizontal' comparison with other beings.

From the Illuminated Wisdom
(al-hikmat an-nuriyah)
in the Word of Joseph

THE Illuminated Wisdom spreads its light in the imaginative Presence (*hadara-t-al-khayâl*), and there is the very beginning of the inspiration (*al-wahî*) in the men of the Divine Assistance (that is to say the messengers and the prophets). 'Aishah (the wife of the Prophet) – May God be Pleased with her! – said : 'the first indication of the Divine Inspiration in God's messenger was the true dream; from then on every dream that he had, appeared like the day which dawns, nothing in it was obscure'; and this state, she added, lasted six months; then came the Angel (who revealed the Koran to him). It is all she understood through her science; she did not know that God's messenger had said : 'people sleep, and when they die they awaken', and all that he saw in the state of wakefulness was of this nature, in spite of the difference of the states (the dream and the wakefulness). She spoke of six months; but in reality, all the earthly existence of the Prophet passed in this way, like a dream in a dream.[1] Now all that is revealed in this manner constitutes the imaginative world (*'âlem al-khayâl*); and it is for that reason that there is symbolism : the reality (*al-amr*) which possesses in itself such and such a 'form'[2] appears under another form; and the interpreter operates in his turn a transposition from the form perceived by the dreamer to the real 'form' of the implied reality, – supposing he guesses it; thus for example, knowledge manifests itself under the appearance of milk; for according to that which was related, the Prophet considered milk as the symbol of knowledge.[3]

[1] His actual dreams, superimposed themselves on the macrocosmic dream, which is the state of wakefulness. Or else, his life unfolded itself as a prophetic dream in the framework of the collective dream, which is the world.

[2] Here as elsewhere, the term 'form' is susceptible to a transposition beyond the world actually 'formal' or individual.

[3] When the Sufi masters affirm that 'the world is imagination' (*al-kawnu*

When the Prophet received the Divine Inspiration, he became unconscious of the sensible, ordinary world; they covered him (with some
material) and (his spirit) withdrew itself from those who were present;
then, when that ceased, he returned to this world. So, he received the
Divine Inspiration in the Imaginative Presence, though one could not
say of him that he slept.[4] In the same way, when the Angel appeared
to him in the form of a man, this apparition was revealed equally from
the Imaginative Presence, for in reality there was no man but an
Angel clothed in human form, and the spectator who possessed the
knowledge passed beyond this form until he perceived the 'real' form.
Thus the Prophet said (of a mysterious stranger, who had come to
question him in front of his companions): 'it was Gabriel, who has
come to teach you your religion'; again, he had said: 'answer the
greetings of this man!' He called him 'man' because of the apparent
form, then he said of him: 'it was Gabriel', transposing the form of the
imaginary man to his original; he said the truth in this case as in the
other, for the apparition was visually true, and it was really Gabriel.

Joseph – May Peace be on him! – said (to his father): 'I have seen
eleven stars with the sun and the moon prostrate themselves before

---

khayâl), they mean by that, that all is illusory, that it has not a proper reality,
but also, that it is constituted of 'images' or of reflections of the eternal realities;
for the imagination (khayâl) considered as a cosmic function corresponds to the
formal environment; the 'world of analogies' ('âlem al-mithâl) which comprises
the subtle and the corporal manifestation, is also called the 'world of imagination' (âlem al-khayâl).

To say that the world is imagination does not then mean, according to the
spirit of Sufism, that its reality is reduced to that of the individual subject, of
which it would be as a projection, but one must, on the contrary, understand
that the imagination, which manifests itself 'subjectively' in the soul of the
individual, possesses if not in its assignation, at least in its structure, a cosmic
character, so is in a way 'objective'. And it must be that it is thus, so that the
'subjective' imagination may reproduce the continuity of the 'great world'; for
it is by the imagination that we realize this world as a continuous atmosphere.
Only when one has realized this cosmic character of the imagination, will one
see at the same time that all the formal world is 'woven of the same cloth', and
in consequence that it is illusory with regard to the Intellect which transcends
the macrocosmic 'imagination' just as it transcends 'subjective' imagination.

[4] Abu Hamid al-Ghazzali affirms that the prophets possess an imaginative
faculty incomparably more powerful than that of other men, which obviously
does not mean that they be particularly subject to illusion, but that their
imagination is up to the standard of the intellectual and spiritual function
which qualifies them as prophets: the revelation 'is fixed' in the sensible order
and more exactly in the imagination which corresponds to it interiorly. One
must know that the revelation (nuzûl) in the proper sense comprises a 'cosmic'

me';[5] he had seen his brothers in the form of stars, and his father and his step-mother in the form of the sun and the moon; it is thus that they appeared from Joseph's point of view; for if the apparition had been real from the point of view of the people appearing in the form of stars, the sun and the moon, it would have been necessary that it was voluntary on their part; but since they were not conscious of it, Joseph's vision took place only in the domain of his imagination; that is why his father Jacob – May Peace be on him! – said to him, when Joseph told him of this vision: 'O my son, do not tell thy vision to thy brothers in case they should practise deceit against thee . . .'[6] then, absolving his sons of this deceit, he transposed it to Satan – who is none other than the very essence of deceit – saying: 'in truth, Satan is the declared enemy of man'.[7] Then, at the end of the story, Joseph said (on receiving his parents and brothers in Egypt): 'This is the interpretation of my dream of long ago, which my Lord has rendered true',[8] that is to say: that He manifested it in tangible form after it had appeared in imaginative form. Now, to this the Prophet answered him: 'the people sleep, (and when they die they waken) . . .' Joseph spoke then like someone who had just awakened from a dream and who interprets it without being conscious that he was still in a state of dreaming, so that he was to say, later, when he really wakened: I dreamt such and such a thing, then, believing I was awake, I dreamt that I interpreted the dream in such a manner . . . It is analogous to that which Joseph said; remark then the difference between the comprehension of Muhammed and that of Joseph, when the latter said, at the end of his adventure: 'this is the interpretation of my dream of long ago which the Lord made real . . .' that is to say sensible; but, it had always been sensible, for the imagination concerns only sensible objects and nothing else.[9] See, then, how excellent are the knowledge and the rank of Muhammed!

---

aspect which distinguishes it from the 'revelation' (*tajallî*) in the sense of a state of consciousness: this is pure 'enstasis', whereas the revelation of a sacred text, for example, is a 'descent' (*nuzûl*) of which the manner is in a way 'objective' and analogous to the creation of the world.

[5] Koran XII, 3.

[6] Koran XII, 4.

[7] Ibid.

[8] Koran XII, 99.

[9] According to the Arab psychology, the imaginative world is part of the sensible order, because it is conceived according to the subtle assignations of the five senses and of the corresponding elements.

I would say still more about the (Imaginative) Presence according to the spirit of Joseph – Peace be on him! – conceived in the Muhammedan spirit, as thou wilst see presently, if God wills. Know that reality so called non-divine, meaning the world, belongs to God like the shadow to the person. The world is then the shadow of God; that is, really, the manner in which the One (*al-wujûd*) attributes Itself to the world; for the shadow exists incontestably in the sensible order, on condition, however, that there is something on which this shadow can project itself; so that if one could remove all support from the shadow, it would no longer sensibly be existent, but only intelligible; that is to say it would be potentially contained in the person on which it depends. The place of manifestation of this Divine shadow that one calls the world is the permanent essences (*a'yân*) of possibilities, (*mumkinât*); it is on them that the shadow projects itself. The shadow is known according as to where the Divine Being projects (His shadow) on these permanent essences of possibilities, and it is by the Divine Name, the Light, (*an-nûr*) that the perception of the shadow takes place. The shadow that projects itself on the immutable essences of possibilities is 'in the image' of the unknown Mystery; dost thou not see that shadows stretch towards the dark, which indicates the unfathomable character which belongs to them according to a certain correspondence between the shadow and the person who projects it?[10] Even if the person is white, his shadow is such (as I have just said). Dost thou not see the mountains far away from the spectator appear darker to him, merely because of their distance, and in spite of their own colour?[11] or, that the sky appears blue? All this is the effect of distance on non-luminous bodies. In the same way the essences of possibilities are not luminous,

[10] This description of the 'shadow of God' recalls that of *Mâyâ* according to the commentators of Vedânta, *Mâyâ* being equally that which manifests the Absolute as multiple at the same time that it hides the true nature; 'one cannot say of it (of *Mâyâ*), neither that it is, nor that it is not!' (Shankarâchârya), for it is unfathomable and known only by its effects. – 'Considered under the aspect *ajñâna* (ignorance), it has for support *Atmâ* (the Supreme Self), at the same time as it hides it, just as a dark room is hidden by the darkness of which it is the support. . . . That which is hidden is the character of the unique reality and the supreme beatitude of *Atmâ*. Only its character of pure intellectual light remains, for us to perceive *ajñâna* itself . . .' (G. Dandoy in *L'Ontologie du Vendânta*). One may observe that here as in the symbolism exposed by Ibn 'Arabi, the 'shadow' logically precedes the Light (*an-nûr*).

[11] According to the Arabic conception, the colour blue approaches black; it is in fact, by its cosmic quality, the colour of insoluble depths.

since they are non-existent; they are unchangeable, but they are not qualified by the being or by existence; for the being is light. As for the luminous bodies, spatial distance makes them appear smaller; so that the eye sees the stars as very small bodies, although they are in reality immensely large; thus, for example, it is known by proofs that the sun is of a volume 166 times plus a quarter plus an eighth greater than the volume of the earth,[12] whereas it appears to the eye about the size of a shield; in that is another effect of distance (analogous to the nature at the same time existent and non-existent of the shadow).

Thou knowest the world in the degree of which one can know the shadows; and thou art ignorant of God in the degree of thine ignorance of the person on whom this shadow depends (which is the world); in so much as He has a shadow, one knows Him; and in so far as one is ignorant of that which this shadow keeps secret of the 'form' of the person who projects it, one is ignorant of God – May He be Exalted! – From which we say that God is known to us in a certain respect, and that He is unknown to us in another respect. 'Dost thou not see thy Lord, how He projects the shadow? If He wished, He would make it permanent . . .'[13] that is to say potential in Himself;[14] it is as if He said : God did not reveal Himself to the possibilities before projecting His shadow, so that it was concerning them that which remains always true (in principle) for them, meaning that they do not appear as such in existence. '. . . Then we made of the sun that which demonstrates it (meaning the shadow) . . .';[15] . . . it is the Divine Name the Light (an-nûr) of which we were talking, and it is that which appears in the visual order, for shadows do not exist in the absence of light; 'Then We retracted it towards Us by an easy way';[16] God retracts the shadow towards Him, because it manifests itself from Him, and 'all reality returns to Him'. It is then Him, and it is other than Him, May He be Exalted! All that thou dost perceive is but the Being of God in the permanent essences of possibilities; so that the Ipseity (huwiyah) (of

---

[12] According to modern astronomy the volume of the sun is 1,300,000 times greater than that of the earth. The argument of Ibn 'Arabi is no less true.

[13] Koran XXV, 47.

[14] To tell the truth, there is no 'potentiality' in the Essence, since potentiality possesses a character at once passive and unintelligible; it is, then, a question here of principial 'indifferentiation' of which the potentiality is like the inversed and 'material' image.

[15] Koran XXV, 47.

[16] Koran XXV, 48.

that which thou seest) is God, it is He who is their being, and in so much as there is a difference of forms, they are the essences of the possibilities; in the same way that there remains always 'shadow' by virtue of the difference of forms, there remains always by this same difference, 'world', or 'other than God'. From its existential unity, the shadow is God Himself, for God is the Unique (al-wâhid), the One (al-ahad); and in respect of the multiplicity of sensible forms, it is the world; – so understand then, and realize what I am explaining to thee! – Since the reality is that which I have just said, the world is illusory (mutawahham), it has not a veritable existence; and it is that which one means by the imagination (encompassing the entire world): that is to say that thou dost imagine that (the world) is an autonomous reality, separated from God and added on, whereas it is in itself nothing.[17] Dost thou not see that in the sensible order the shadow is attached to the person who projects it and it is impossible that it can detach itself? For it is inconceivable that a thing can separate itself from its own essence (dhât). Acknowledge then, thine own essence ('ayn), who thou art, what is thine ipseity, what is thy relation towards God – May He be Exalted! – by what thou art God and by what thou art 'world' or 'the other', or whatever corresponds to these expressions, – for such is thy nature. It is with regard to this (meaning this knowledge of thyself) that the wise ones are superior, the ones to the others.

God is, in His relation towards a particular shadow, small or large and more or less pure, like the light in respect of a filter of coloured glass, which tints the light to its own colour whereas it is itself without colour; it is thus that thou canst see the Divine Light; and there lies the symbol of thy reality with regard to thy Lord. But, if thou sayest, on seeing It: 'it is a green light', because the filter is green, thou wilt be right, as the visual experience proves; but if thou sayest that It is not green and It has no colour (in Itself), as reason proves,[18] thou wilt tell

---

[17] Here Ibn 'Arabi stretches the sense of al-khayâl beyond the imaginative world in the strict cosmic sense, for he says of all the cosmos that it is 'imagination' (khayâl), to signify that it is 'illusory' (mutawahham), that it is nothing that can be really outside of God. In this case the sense of the two terms khayâl and wahm correspond exactly to that which the Vêdântines designated as Mâyâ, the 'imagination' corresponding to the idea of 'Divine art' which Mâyâ implies, and the 'conjectural power' (al-wahm) in its aspect of 'avidyâ', that is to say of 'ignorance' or adhyâsâ, of false 'super position'.

[18] We may observe that the sensible perception corresponds to the point of view of analogy or symbolism (tashbîh), whereas reasoning corresponds to the point of view of the transcendence (tanzîh).

the truth, and the argument (extracted from sensible experience) will confirm it.[19]

It is thus that the light projects itself through the shadow, which is none other than the filter, and which is luminous by its transparency. Such also is the man having realized God; the 'form' of God will manifest itself in him more directly than it will manifest itself in others. For there exists among us someone for whom God is his hearing, his sight, his faculties and his organs, according to the signs which the Prophet gave in his message from God; and in spite of that, the determination of the shadow subsists since the possessive pronoun of hearing (and other faculties) are related to it (according to the sacred message: 'I will be *his* hearing by which he hears, *his* sight by which he sees', etc.) Other servants of God are not like this; the servant in question has a more immediate relation towards the Being of God than others have.

Now, as Reality is such as we have affirmed, know that thou art imagination and that all thou perceivest and that thou doth designate as 'other than me' is imagination; for all existence is imagination in imagination (that is to say 'subjective' or microcosmic imagination in an 'objective' collective or macrocosmic imagination); whereas the veritable Being is God alone and exclusively, in respect of His Essence (*dhât*) and of His essential determination (*'ayn*), not in respect of His Names, for His Names have a double significance; on one hand they contain a unique significance, that is to say the essential determination of God, who is the 'named', and on the other hand their significance make it so that each Name distinguishes itself from the others, the Forgiving from the Apparent, the Apparent from the Interior, and so on; but, what then is the connection between one Name and another? for thou wilt have understood that each Name is the essential determination of every other; in so far as one name is the essential determination of the other, it is God, and in so far as it differs, it is the 'imaginary' God, as we have exposed. Exalted may He be who is proved only by Himself and who exists only by His own unchangeable Essence! There is in existence only that which denotes Unity; and there is in imagination only that which denotes multiplicity. So, whoever belongs to multiplicity, is in the world, with the Divine Names and with

[19] This symbolism corresponds exactly to the advaïtine theory of pure light (*bimba*) of the Self (*Atmâ*) decomposed by the filter of *Mâyâ* in diversely coloured light (*pratibimba*).

the names of the world; and whoever belongs to Unity, is with God in respect of His Essence 'independent of worlds'. If the Essence 'is independent of worlds', it means that God must be essentially independent of 'nominal relations', for the Names do not denote the Essence only, they denote at the same time other realities, of which they define the manifestation. 'Say: He, God, is One (*ahad*)' – In His Essence – 'God is Absolute' – the independent upon which everything depends, – 'He does not beget' – neither in His aseity, nor in His relation towards us (that is to say towards our principial non-existence) – 'and He is not begotten', – in the same respect – 'and there is no equal to Him' – in this respect.[20] It is that which is His own quality; by His word: 'say: He, God, is one . . .' He abstracts His Essence from all multiplicity; on the other hand, this manifests itself by virtue of the well known Divine Attributes. It is we who beget and are begotten, and it is we who depend on Him – May He be Exalted! – so we are similar one to another, whereas the Unique, the Transcendent, is independent with regard to these attributes just as He is independent of us. There is no other adequate description of God than this 'surat', the 'surat' of Purity (*al-ikhlâs*), and it is as such that it was revealed (that is to say as answer to the question of the Jews; 'describe us Thy Lord, how He is'.)

The Unity of God which reveals itself in respect of the Divine Names, postulating our existence is the unity of the multiple (*ahadiyat al-kuthrah*), and the Unity of God by which He is independent of us and of the Names, is the essential Unity; the one and the other are contained in the Name the One (*al-ahad*).

Know then that if God manifested the shadows, and if He made them 'prostrate themselves and bend to the right and to the left' ('Do they not see each thing that God hath created, how its shadow inclines to the right and to the left, prostrating itself before God . . .' Koran XVI 48) it is because He wanted to give thee signs with regard to thyself and Himself, so that thou knowest who thou art, what is thy relation towards Him and His relation towards you, so that thou knowest by what, or by virtue of what Divine reality that which is 'other than God' is qualified by complete indigence, (*faqr*) towards God, as well as relative indigence, that is to say, by a mutual dependence of its own parts, and so that thou knowest by what and by virtue of what essential reality God qualified Himself with independence with regard to

[20] Koran CXII. Surat of the Purity.

men and by independence with regard to worlds, whereas the world is qualified by relative independence, that is to say that each of its parts is in a certain sense independent of the other, as it is also, according to a different sense to this one dependent on the other; for the world depends incontestably on causes, its supreme cause being its Divine causability; and there is no other Divine causability on which the world would depend other than the Divine Names; the world depends on each of the Divine Names, both in virtue of that which is analogous to such a Name in this world, and because each Name is contained in the essential determinations of God, for it is God and nothing else. For that He says 'you are the indigent (*fuqarâ*) towards God, and it is He, God, the Rich, the Glorious'.[21] On the other hand it is evident that we depend the one on the other.

Our own 'names' are in reality but the Divine Names, since everything depends on Him. As for our own essences (*a'yân*), they are in reality His 'shadow', no more. For He is our ipseity, just as He is not our ipseity. – Here, we have just prepared the way for thee!

[21] Koran XXXV, 15.

From the Wisdom of the Prophecy
(al-hikmat an-nubûwiyah)
in the Word of Jesus ('Aissa)

THE Spirit (ar-rûh : that is to say Christ) was manifested by the water
    of Mary and the breath of Gabriel;
In the form of a man made of clay,
In the purified body of (corruptible) nature that he calls 'prison' –
    (sijîn).
So that he is staying there since more than a thousand years.[1]
A 'spirit of God' :[2] of no other :
It is for that that he resuscitated the dead and created the bird from
    clay.[3]
His relation towards his Lord is such,
That he acts through it in superior and inferior worlds.
God purified his body and elevated him in spirit,
And made of him the symbol of His act of creation.[4]

Know that spirits have the virtue of communicating life to all that
they touch. It is for this reason, that as-Sâmirî[5] (of whom it is said in
the Koran that he made the golden calf which the Israelites wor-

---

[1] That is to say the time passed since the ascension of Christ until the
moment that this book was written; he will remain there until his 'second
coming' at the end of the cycle.

[2] . . . . The Messiah, Jesus, son of Mary, is the apostle of God, and His
Word, which He projected unto Mary, and a spirit proceeding from Him.'
(Koran IV, 170).

[3] '(Jesus will say unto them): I come to show you the signs of your Lord;
I will mould of clay the figure of a bird, and I will blow on it, and it will
be a (living) bird, by permission of God. . . .' (Koran III, 43). The story of
the child Jesus giving life to a bird of clay is also found in the apocryphal
gospels.

[4] Since Christ resurrected the dead.

[5] The significance of this Koranic name is not clear; some have translated
it as the 'samaritan' which is an anachronism only too evident.

shipped during the absence of Moses),[6] seized of the dust in the traces
of the (Divine) messenger, who was (the Archangel) Gabriel; for as-
Sâmirî knew this virtue of the spirits, and when he learnt that the
messenger was Gabriel, he knew that life was communicated to the
place where he had struck his foot; so he picked up a handful of dust[7]
and threw it in the (golden) calf, which 'lowed' at once in the manner
of the bovine: the statue would have emitted the voice of no matter
what other animal, including man, if it had had that form. This power
comes from the life infused into things, life which one calls *lâhût*,
(Divine Nature), whereas the recipient to which the spirit gives life is
called *nâsût* (human nature); and this *nâsût* (which contains the corporal form) is in its turn considered as a spirit because of that which
maintains it in existence.[8]

When the 'faithful Spirit' (*ar-rûh al-âmîn*), who is Gabriel, appeared
to Mary 'in the form of harmonious man' she imagined that he was a
man trying to know her carnally, and knowing that it was not permitted, she 'took refuge in God against him'[9] with all her being, consequently she was overwhelmed with a perfect state of the Divine
Presence, a state which was identical with the Intellectual Spirit (*ar-rûh
al ma'nâwî*). If Gabriel had blown his breath into her at the time that
she was in this state, Jesus would have been born such that nobody
could tolerate him because of his uncompromising nature, conforming
to the state of his mother at the time of his conception. But as soon as
Gabriel said to Mary: 'In truth, I am the messenger of your Lord,
and have come to give thee a pure son',[10] she relaxed from her state of

---

[6] '(The Israelites said to Moses): We have not failed in what we promised
thee of our own authority; but we were ordered to collect our ornaments . . .
in loads. As-Sâmirî cast them (in the fire) and produced for the people a
corporal calf, which lowed. . . .' Koran XX, 90.

[7] '(Moses said): And thou, O, as-Sâmirî!; what was thy design? He
answered: I saw that which they saw not, I took a handful of dust from the
footsteps of the messenger of God, and I cast it into the molten calf, for
so did my mind direct me' (Koran XX, 96).

[8] This passage seems to allude to the two natures of Christ. These may be
considered as two aspects of his Spirit or of his Essence.

[9] '. . . . We sent our Spirit unto her and he appeared unto her in the shape
of a harmonious man. She said: I seek refuge in God from thee; if thou
fearest Him. . . .' (Koran XIX, 17, 18).

[10] 'He answered: I am the messenger of thy Lord, and am sent to give
thee a pure son. – She said, how shall I have a son? For no man hath touched
me and I do not transgress. He replied: It is thus that thy Lord hath said:
This is easy for me; He will be Our symbol for men, and a mercy from Us.
The order is decreed. . . .' (Koran XIX, 19–21)

contraction and her breast swelled; and it is then that Gabriel blew into her (the spirit) of Jesus. Gabriel – Peace be on him! – was, then, the vehicle of the Divine Word transmitted to Mary, in the same way as the messenger (*ar-rasûl*) transmitted the words of God to his people, according to the Koranic word: '(Jesus was) His Word that He projected into Mary, and the Spirit from Him'.[11] From that instant loving desire flooded Mary, so that the body of Jesus was created from the veritable 'water' (or seed) of Mary and of the purely imaginary 'water' (or seed) of Gabriel, transmitted by the humidity principially inherent in breath – for the breath of the living contains the element of water. Thus the body of Jesus was constituted of imaginary 'water' and of real 'water', and he was born a child in the human form because of his mother and because of the apparition of Gabriel in the form of a man; since there is no one generated in this human species, outside the usual order.[12]

In the same way, Jesus resuscitated the dead because he is the Divine Spirit – God alone gives life; whereas the breath (which transmitted life) was from Jesus; just as the breath blown into Mary was the breath of Gabriel, whereas the Word came from God. In this way the resuscitation of the dead is really an action of Jesus since it emanated from his breath, just as he himself emanated from the form of his mother; on the other hand, it is only in appearance that the resuscitation was performed by him, seeing that it is essentially a Divine Act. Jesus united in himself these two realities, by virtue of his constitution, of which we were saying that it is the issue at once of imaginary seed (or created by the power of suggestion: *al-wahm* and a real seed: so that the action of resuscitating the dead comes from him in a manner which is effective on the one hand, and supposed on the other. According to the former of these aspects, it is said of him: 'he vivifies the dead',[13] and according to the latter aspect: 'he breathes into him (that is to say into the bird made of clay) and he becomes a bird by the

---

[11] Koran IV, 170.

[12] That is to say that the miracle does not abolish the natural order but summarizes it incidentally in its superior principle; here, the spiritual power of Gabriel summarizes the corporal order in its subtle principle without the polarity of the specific generation being destroyed by it. – All this cosmological explanation of the conception of Jesus is not given with the purpose of making relative the Divine intervention; it should make the constitution itself of Christ be understood, the exceptional connection which relates his 'paternal' element to his 'maternal' substance, as will be shown in the text that follows.

[13] Koran III, 48.

permission of God',[14] the agent, in this case, being logically attached
to the expression : 'by the permission of God'; – that is to say that the
transformation of the bird of clay to the real bird was done by the
intervention of God; however one can also attach the Divine permission
to the act of blowing and not to the transformation (of the form in
clay) into a bird (of whom the specific soul), would then be simply due
to the apparent form (of the object which received the life-giving
breath). It is the same for the curing of the blind-born and the lepers
and for every other miraculous action attributed (according to the
Koran) to Jesus on the one hand, and the permission of God on the
other; permission given to the first or the second person, according to
the Koranic words : 'by My permission' or 'by the permission of
God'.[15] So, if the permission of God is with regard to the blowing, the
bird was created, with the Divine permission, by he who blew in (the
clay object). On the other hand, if the action of blowing does not
depend (directly) on the Divine permission, it is the transformation of
the bird (of clay) to a (real) bird which will depend on it, and the agent
of this transformation is then implied in the term : 'he becomes'. If
the act in question did not carry in itself something effective and something imaginary, the event could not assume indifferently the two
aspects; and it is thus because the constitution of Jesus contains in itself
the one and the other aspect.

Jesus manifested humility so far as to order his community that they
humble themselves when giving alms, and if someone is struck on his
cheek, he offers the other to he who has struck him and does not turn
against him nor seek vengeance. This Jesus took from the side of his
mother, for it is to the woman to submit quite naturally, since the
woman is legally and physically subject to man. His powers of resurrection and of healing, on the other hand, came to him from the
breath of Gabriel invested in human form. It is from that that Jesus
could revive the dead while having the form of a man. If Gabriel had
not appeared (to Mary) in human form but under any other sensible
form, animal, vegetable or mineral, Jesus would not have resurrected
the dead without, at that moment, having assumed this non-human
form, and become manifested in it; in the same way, if Gabriel had
appeared in a form of (spiritual) light exempt from the sensible
elements and qualities – although contained in the Universal Nature

[14] Koran III, 48.
[15] Koran V, 110.

[71]

(*at-tabî 'ah*), – Jesus would not have resurrected the dead without appearing, himself, at the time of his action, in this form of supra-sensible light, still assuming the human form that he received from his mother's side. Because of that (that is to say, because of his identification with Gabriel, at the time of the miraculous act), it was said of him, when he resurrected the dead, that it was him and yet not him, and the spectators were amazed as they watched him, just as he who reflects on this action is amazed at a human person who revives the dead, whereas it is a Divine property to revive things bestowed of the Word – not the other animals (these participating, in a way, in the life of the Perfect Man); the thinker is confused to see a Divine action emanating from a human form. It is that which caused some to solicit the 'localisation' (*hulûl*) of God (in the human nature of Jesus), and others to say that Jesus was God in so far as he revived the dead, and for that the Koran attributes to them the '*kufr*' (disbelief) a word which signifies literally the veil (*sitr*), because they 'veil' God, who, He, really revives the dead through the human form of Jesus. God says (in the Koran): 'these are unbelievers who say: in truth, God is Himself the Messiah, son of Mary',[16] for they accumulated the deviation and disbelief in their affirmation, not because they said that the Messiah was God, nor in naming him the son of Mary, but since they identified God, in so far as he resurrected the dead, with the human terrestial form expressly appointed as the son of Mary. Certainly, Jesus was the son of Mary; and whoever hears the phrase in question could believe that they were attributing the Divine Nature (*al-ulûhiyah*) to the form of Jesus in the sense that the Divinity is the essence of this form; but it is nothing of the sort, since they made of the Divine Ipseity (*al-huwiyah*) the subject of the human form appointed to be the son of Mary (by the expression: 'God is Himself, etc.'); they distinguished, then, the (human) form as such from the source (of which it is a manifestation) and did not identify the form (of Christ) essentially to this principle (which manifests itself by the resurrection of the dead),[17] just as one distinguishes the human form which Gabriel assumed, from the breath which he instilled into Mary; for although the breath emanated from this form, it does not essentially flow from it.

[16] Koran V, 19.

[17] That is to say, they defined the form of Jesus as human terrestrial form by the words: 'Son of Mary', at the same time identifying God in this form. It is a question, clearly, of the confusion of the two natures, divine and human, of Christ.

From this, different religious communities contradict each other on the subject of Jesus' identity – Peace be on him! – certain, considering him by virtue of his terrestrial form, affirmed that he was the son of Mary;[18] others, envisaging in him the apparently human form, attach him to Gabriel; and still others, because the resurrection of the dead emanated from him, attached him to God by the Spirit, saying of him that he was the Spirit of God, meaning that it was he who communicated life to whoever received his breath. Thus, each in turn, one sees in him either God, or the Angel, or human nature; so that he is for each spectator whatever the spectator imposes on himself; he is the Word of God, he is the Spirit of God, and he is the servant (that is to say the creature) of God. This is something that has taken place for no other man, in so far as one considers his apparent form. For each person attaches himself naturally to his formal father and not to he who breathed his spirit into the human form. For when God 'forms' as He says it, the human body, and into it He then 'blows' His Spirit,[19] this Spirit is related, by its existence and by its essence, to God alone. But, for Jesus, it is not thus, the preparation of his body and of his form being implied in the spiritual breath (that Gabriel projected into Mary). Such is not the case for other human beings (but the preparation of the body precedes the inspiration of the spirit) as we have just said.

All existences are 'the Words of God which are inexhaustable';[20] for all are but the word 'Be!' (kun) which is the Word of God. Now must one believe that the Word is related immediately to God in His principial state? If it is thus, it is impossible for us to know its quiddity; or, is it that God 'descends' to the form of he who says: 'Be', so that this word 'Be' is the Essential Reality (al-haqîqah) of the form towards which God 'descends', or in which He manifests Himself. Some men of God assert the former, and others the latter, and still others are

[18] Ibn 'Arabi does not consider Mary under the aspect of Theotokos 'Mother of God'; this expression even, would be completely unintelligible from the point of Islam, which always distinguishes clearly between the created and the uncreated; the idea of 'God manifested', in the direct and concrete sense of this term, is however to be found in Sufism, that is to say in the identification of the Name of God with God Himself.

[19] 'When I shall have formed him, and I shall have breathed of My Spirit into him. . . .' (Koran XV, 29).

[20] 'Say: If the sea were ink to write the words of my Lord, verily the sea would fail, before the supply of words from my Lord would fail, even if We produced again as much ink' (Koran XVIII, 109).

disconcerted by the ambiguity of the aspects. This question can only be resolved by intuition. Abu-Yazîd who blew on the ant that he had killed (inadvertently), and brought it back to life, knew quite well by whom he blew and that it was through Him that he blew; his contemplation was Christ-like.

As for the vivification through knowledge, that is Divine Life, essential, superior, luminous, of which God said (in the Koran); '. . . or he who was dead and whom We resurrected, giving him light by which he walks among the people . . .'[21] Whosoever revives a dead soul by the life of knowledge in no matter which domain related to the Knowledge of God, really vivifies, this particular knowledge being for this soul like a light with which he walks among the people, that is to say amongst those who are of the same form as he.

'Without Him (as active principal) and without us (as receptacles of
      His act) nothing would exist.
I adore Him truly;
And God is our Master.
But I am He Himself ('*Aynuh*)
For so much as thou considereth (in me) the (Universal) Man,
Then do not let thyself be blinded by the veil of the individual man,
And he will be for thee an evident symbol.
Be at once God (in thine essence) and creature (by thy form)
And thou wilt be through God the dispenser of His grace.
Nourish His creation through Him,
Thou wilt be a 'reviving rest and a scent of life' (*rawhân wa raihânâ*).[22]
(As determinations) We give Him that by which He manifests Himself
      in us; Whereas He gives us the being.
So that the Act (*al-amr*) belongs at once to Him and to us.
He who knew by my heart, at the time when He gave us life, revives
      it (by knowledge).[23]
We were in Him, existences, determinations and the relations of time.
This state (of the contemplation of our permanent possibilities in God)
      does not persist in us,
But it is that which gave us life.'

[21] Koran VI, 122.
[22] Koran LVI, 88.
[23] This verse may also be translated in the following manner: He who knew Him by my heart, at the hour that He gave us life, bestowed on Him individual life.

[74]

That which we were saying about the Spiritual Breath working through the human terrestial form is to be found corroborated by the fact that God attributes to Himself the 'breath of Clemency' (*an-nafas ar-rahmânî*). Now the attribution of a quality necessarily involves everything that (the symbolism of) this quality contains; in the present case, thou knowest well that which the (animal) breath contains (elementary characters such as expansion, propagation, the production of sound, etc). That is why one says that the Divine Breath englobes all the forms of the world; in fact, it is for them like the Materia Prima (*al-jawhar al-hayûlanî*), which is nothing but the first determination of Universal Nature (*at-tabî 'ah*). The four elements[24] are but the forms, among others, of all those that it contains; that which is above the elements and above everything that is constituted by the elements, is equally a part, in so much as 'forms', of the Universal Nature; that is to say that not only the spirits and the essences of the seven celestial spheres,[25] but also the 'superior spirits' (*al-malâ al-a'lâ*) are issued from Universal Nature; it is because of that, moreover, that God describes them as rivalling the ones with the others; for Nature comprises the polarization; the opposition of the Divine Names – which are the (universal) relations – the one to the others come precisely from 'the Breath of Clemency'; whereas the Essence (*adh-dhât*), which is not submitted to this (polarizing) condition, is 'independent of the worlds'. As for the world, it was produced 'in the form' of its manifesting principle, which is no other than the Divine Breath.[26]

The Divine Breath 'arises' by virtue of the heat which is inherent to it, it 'descends' by virtue of cold and humidity, and 'fixes itself' and 'solidifies' by virtue of dryness. The 'precipitation' (of the common world) comes, then, from cold and from humidity (that is to say that which corresponds to these qualities in the universal order); just as one can verify in medicine : to administer a medicine to accelerate the digestion, the doctor waits until he observes a precipitation in the water of the patient, a precipitation which comes about by a predominance, in the organism, of natural cold and humidity.

Moreover (the primordial polarization which qualifies Universal

[24] Considered as four 'natural' foundations of the subtle world and the corporal world, at the same time.
[25] Which are 'elementary' because they participate in subtle modalities of the four elements.
[26] According to this conception, the Universal Nature – or Divine Breath – is analogous to that of the Hindu doctrine designated as the *Shakti* or as *Mâyâ*.

Nature is symbolized by the fact that God) moulds the clay of man 'with His two hands' which are evidently opposed the one to the other; although each one of them may be in a certain sense, as one has said, a 'right hand', their distinction is never the less real, be it only because there are two of them. For Nature, which comprises opposition, is governed only by that which corresponds to it. Moreover, it is by this kneading of His two hands that God called man *bashar*,[27] this word alluding to the 'tenderness' (*al-mubâsharah*) which was lavished on man by the two Divine hands which fashioned him; that which signifies a particular Divine favour for the human species, for (according to the Koran) God said to he who refused to prostrate himself before Adam : 'What prevents thee from prostrating thyself before that which I have created with My two hands? Art thou proud (towards that which is thy equal, that is to say he who is made of elements like thee), or art thou one of the Superior beings (*al-'alîn*)',[28] – who, they, exceed the domain of the element which is however not thy case! We mean, then, by superior spirits those who, from their essence and in their luminous nature, rise above the elements, while still depending on Universal Nature. Man surpasses the other species of the elementary domain only because he is 'kneaded' by the Divine 'Two Hands'; it is from that that his species is more noble than any other species formed by the elements without this double Divine touch (which corresponds to the 'central' nature of man); that is to say that man possesses a dignity superior to that of the terrestrial angels (amongst whom are the genii) as also the celestial angels (populating the seven celestial spheres, formed of subtle modalities of the elements), whereas the superior angels are better than the human species, according to the sacred text (since they did not have to prostrate themselves before Adam).

He who wants to know the Divine Breath (*nafas*), let him consider the world; for (according to the Word of the Prophet) 'he who knows his self (*nafsahu*), knows his Lord' who manifests Himself in him; I mean that the world is manifested in the Breath of the Clement, by which God 'dilated' (*naffasa*) the possibilities implied in the Divine Names, relieving them (*naffasa*) so to speak from the restraint of the state of non-manifestation; and doing this, He was generous towards Himself (*nafsahu*) because He manifests in Himself (*fî-nafsihi*); so that it is from that side that is affirmed the first action of the Divine Breath

[27] Koran XV, 28.
[28] Koran XXXVIII, 75.

(*an-nafas*). From then on, the Divine Act does not cease to descend gradually by the 'alleviation (*tanfîs*) of anguish'[29] until the last of the manifestations.

'All is contained in the Divine Breath
Like the day in the morning's dawn.
The knowledge transmitted by demonstration is like the dawn for
     he who drowses;
So that he sees that which I have said, as a dream, symbol of the
     Divine Breath,
Which, after the shadows, consoles him of all distress.
He has long ago revealed Himself to he who came to fetch a fire-
     brand,
And who saw Him as a fire, whereas He is a Light in the (spiritual)
     kings and in the 'travellers',
If thou understandeth my words thou knowest that thou hast need
     (of the apparent form) :
If (Moses) had searched for something other (than the fire)
He would have seen Him in that, and not inversely.'

As for the words which Jesus answered (according to the Koran) to a certain question that God posed to him (in the same connection as to that which made Him say elsewhere : 'We will try them until we know'), – I mean, as if He wanted to know if a certain thing that was attributed to Jesus had really happened or not and that although He knew it from all eternity), in saying to him : 'Hast thou said to the people that they should take thee and thy mother for Divinities beside Me?'[30] the reply had to conform to the connection and to the aspect under which the questioner was revealed : now, Wisdom demanded, in this case, that the answer respected the duality essentially contained in the Unity; and it is for that that Jesus said – first exalting God above the forms and defining Him at the same time by the pronoun of the second person, which indicates the confrontation : – 'May Thou be Exalted, it is not to me' – that is to say, to my ego which is distinguished from Thee – 'to say that which is not mine according to the Truth' – from my identity or from my individual essence – 'if I said it;

---

[29] According to the doctrine of the Greek fathers, the world was created 'by the Son (the Word) in the Holy Spirit', that which is also called the 'Consoler'.

[30] 'And when God said unto Jesus: Hast thou ever said unto men: Take me

[77]

Thou knewest it'; – for in reality it is Thou who spoke, and he who speaks knows what he says; Thou art the tongue by which I speak; (as we were taught by the Messenger of God, May Peace be on him, in reporting the Divine Message' : . . . and I am the tongue by which he speaks, etc', God thus identifying Himself essentially to the tongue of the chosen one who speaks, the word coming from the individual). Afterwards, the saintly servant (Jesus), said, in continuing his answer : 'Thou knowest that which is in me', – and it is implicitly God who speaks, – 'and I, I do not know what there is in Thee', that is to say, I do not know that which is in the Ipseity : this word denies only the knowledge of the Aseity (*al-huwiyah*) as such (in its infinity) and not in so much as it is the author of the words and acts (of Jesus). 'In truth, it is Thee (the One who knows the secrets)'; by the pronoun Thou he emphasized the distinction, God alone (in His infinity) knowing all the secrets. It is thus that he separated (the individual from His Divine Essence) and united (the two, saying 'If I said it, Thou knewest it . . .'); he affirmed the Unity of God, and the multiplicity (that it implies); he envisaged the universal and the particular at the same time.

He said in ending his reply 'I did not say anything to them except that which Thou hast ordered me to tell them'; he started by negation,

---

and my mother for two Divinities, beside God? He replied: Praise be unto Thee! it is not for me to say that which I have not the right to say (or: that which is not, according to me, the truth). If I had said so Thou wouldst surely have known it; Thou knowest what is in me, but I know not what is in Thee, for Thou art the Knower of Secrets. I did not say anything to them except that which thou didst command me to say: Worship God, my Lord and your Lord. As long as I was living among them I was their witness, but since Thou hast taken me to Thyself, Thou hast been the Watcher over them, for Thou art Witness to all things. If Thou punisheth them, they are Thy servants; and if Thou forgive them, Thou art Mighty and Wise. – God said: This day shall their veracity be of advantage unto those who speak the truth; they shall have gardens where rivers shall flow, they shall remain there for ever. God will be well pleased in them, and they will be well pleased in God. This shall be great felicity'. (Koran V, 115-118). It is to be observed that the expression 'Divinities beside God', at the beginning of this Koranic passage, defines very exactly the error which, without being justified by the Christian doctrine, may practically be introduced in the cult of the 'Son of God' and of the 'Mother of God'. By reason of the abuse arisen in the breast of Christianity, the Koran affirms the Divine Transcendance. The symbolism of the Theotokos is however, implicitly confirmed in the following Koranic passage: 'We made of the son of Mary, and his mother (that is to say the mother of Jesus) a sign. We prepared an abode for them in an elevated place, tranquil, (or immutable) and abundant in springs' (Koran XXIII, 49).

alluding to the fact he had no (separate) existence; then, he compensated this negation by his affirmation with regard to his questioner; if he had not acted in this way, he would have ignored the Divine Truths – and far from him such ignorance! – He says, then: '. . . except that which Thou hast ordered me', since it is Thou that speaketh with my tongue, since Thou art my tongue itself. Observe this consideration of the Divine and spiritual polarity (of the Divine Act and of he who receives it); what could there be more subtle! '(I have not told them anything except that which Thou hast ordered me to tell them:) adore God'; he employed the name of God (*Allâh*) because of the different points of view of the adorers and because of the difference of the cults, this Name (*Allâh*) comprising all the Divine Aspects without affirming a single one of them in particular; and he added: 'my Lord and your Lord', for it is certain that the relationship that makes of the Divinity, the Lord of such and such a manifested being is something exclusive; and it is because of that that he distinguished between 'my Lord' and 'your Lord' by the respective pronouns. By the words: '. . . except only that which Thou hast ordered me' he describes himself as he who submits to the Order (*al-amr*), which corresponds to his state of (perfect) servant, for no one receives Orders who is not expected to execute them, even if he is unable to carry them out.

Since the Divine Order (or the Act) reveals itself in conformity to the hierarchy of Existence, all that which appears to whatever degree of this hierarchy colours itself according to the proper reality of this degree. The degree of he who submits to the Order (or the Act) implies a certain condition which appears in everyone who receives an order; in the same way, the degree of the Order (or of the Act) implies a condition appearing in all that which orders (or acts). Thus, God said: 'accomplish the prayer!' In which He is the Ordering One, while the one obliged in the cult receives the Order; on the other hand, the adorer says: 'Lord, forgive me!' And this time it is he who is ordering, while God receives the order. Now, that which God demands by His Order from the adorer is no more than that which the adorer asks by his demand from God; and it is for that, moreover, that all prayer is granted, even if the reply is retarded. In the same way; it so happens that certain adorers, who have received the Divine Order to accomplish the prayer at a certain hour, retard it, and accomplish it only at the hour at which they are able; in this case, equally, the obedience to the Order is postponed, although it must certainly take place (on the part of the real adorer), be it only by intention alone (to accomplish the rite ordered).

When Jesus said 'I was their witness' – by that he does not imply himself, as he did in saying 'my Lord' and 'your Lord' – 'as long as I lived among them'; for the Prophets are the witnesses of their communities as long as they live : 'but when Thou hast gathered me', – that is to say, when Thou raised me to Thee and Thou hast hidden me from them, and hidden them from me, – 'Thou wast their observer' – no longer through my substance, but in their own substances, since Thou wert their own interior regard who observed them; for the consciousness that a man has of himself is the consciousness of God towards him. Jesus designated God by the Name of the Observer (*ar-raqîb*) after having designated himself as the Witness (*ash-shahîd*), to mark the difference between him and his Lord, so that one knew that he considered himself as servant and God as his own Lord. But, know that to God, the Observer, belongs also the name that Jesus, according to his word; 'I was their witness' attributed to himself, for Jesus also said 'And it is Thou who art the Witness of all things'; he says 'thing' (*shay*) in the sense of a negation of negations, so that the expression 'all things' comprises absolutely everything; and he employed the divine Name the Witness in the sense that God contemplates the proper and essential reality of all things. By that he indicated that God Himself was the Witness of the community of Jesus, of which he had said : 'I was their witness, as long as I lived among them'; it relates to the Divine Witness in the substance of Jesus, according to the well-known Divine Message, which affirms that God is the tongue and the hearing and the sight (of the chosen one). Then he pronounced a word which is at the same time of Jesus and of Muhammed; of Jesus, because it is to him that it is attributed by the Divine Writing; it is to Muhammed because he pronounced it on a certain occasion and he read it an entire night, without turning to anything else, until dawn : 'If Thou punisheth them, they are Thy servants; and if Thou pardoneth them, it is Thou the Powerful, the Wise'. The pronoun 'they' like the pronoun 'he', expresses the actual absence of he of whom one speaks; and in this case, the absence of those of whom Jesus said : 'If Thou punisheth them,' etc., is like the veil which hid God from them. It is thus that Jesus reminded them of God before they appeared before Him, so that the leaven might have acted on the dough, by the time they would appear before God, and that the dough (their receptive

substance) might then become equal to the leaven (their spiritual consciousness). In saying : 'they are Thy servants' he affirms that it is God
alone that they adored : at the same time, he proves their extreme state
of humiliation, for nobody is more humiliated than the servant or slave
(al-'abd) who does not act by himself but depends entirely on the law
which is imposed by his unique Lord. In calling them 'Thy servants'
(or slaves), he expresses the exclusive Lordship (of God on them); now,
the punishment signifies humiliation; but they are already humiliated
to the extreme by being slaves; their very nature implies humiliation;
(it is as if he said) : 'Thou doth not humiliate them more than by the
fact that they are Thy slaves. And if Thou pardoneth them', – that is
to say, if Thou coverth them and protecteth them from the punishment they have attracted, – 'It is Thou the Powerful (al-'azîz)' – that
is the protector. (When God confers the Name al-'azîz (which also
means the 'Loved', 'the Dear', 'the Precious') on one of His servants,
God becomes Himself the Lover towards this servant and defends him
from the interference of the Name the Vengeful, from whence comes
punishment.)

On the other hand, Jesus distinguished the Divinity from the
creature, recapitulating moreover this distinction by the analogous
affirmations, like : 'it is Thou the Knower of the Secrets', 'it is Thou
who wert their Observer . . .', and : 'it is Thou the Powerful, the Wise'.

The words : 'if Thou punisheth them,' etc., becomes, on the lips of
the Prophet, an instant request, for he repeated it to his Lord during
an entire night, until the breaking of dawn, imploring a reply. If he
had heard the answer since the first request, he would not have insisted; but God showed him bit by bit the reasons for which they
merited punishment, and the Prophet said to Him each time : 'If Thou
punisheth them, they are Thy servants; and if Thou pardoneth them,
it is Thou the Powerful, the Wise'; if he could have known towards
which way the Divine decision was inclining, he would have asked forgiveness for them in the sense indicated; however, God showed him
only, conforming to the verse recited, their dependence on the Divine
Pardon. According to the words of the Prophet, God, when He loves
the voice of His servant who prays to Him, defers the granting of the
prayer, so that the servant may repeat his prayer, and He acts thus by
love, not because He is turned away from him. For this reason, Jesus
mentioned the Name the Wise (al-hakîm) for this Name denotes he
who puts everything in its place and does not remain indifferent to

that which reality requires from each thing by virtue of its (particular) qualities; the wise one, then, is he who knows the order of things. In repeating this verse of the Koran, the Prophet was contemplating an immense knowledge which God had given him; let anyone who recites this verse be conscious of it, or remain quiet! When God obliges some-one to persist in a prayer, He does it only in view of granting it and satisfying his need. Let nobody, then, renounce the prayer that has been assigned to him, but let him persist with the endurance which the Messenger of God had in reciting this verse, in every state, until he hears the reply with his ears or with his hearing – as thou wilt, or as God will make him understand. If God accords thee the prayer from the tongue, He will make thee understand His answer by ear; and if He accords the prayer by the spirit He will make thee hear His answer by thy hearing.

The Wisdom of the Merciful Beatitude
(al-hikmat ar-rahmâniyah)
in the Word of Solomon

BILQÎS said: 'In truth it is from Solomon, and it is in the Name of God, the Clement (ar-rahmân), the Merciful (ar-rahîm)';[1] that means: 'In truth, this letter is from Solomon, and its contents are: in the Name of God, the Clement, the Merciful . . .' Certain people wanted to deduce (from this Koranic passage) that Solomon had placed his own name before that of God; but it is nothing of the sort, for it would be inconsistent with the knowledge that Solomon had of his Lord; and how would it be thus, when Bilqîs said herself: 'a noble (or generous) letter has just been brought to me . . .', that is to say a letter that honoured her? Perhaps the people were influenced in their interpretation by the story of the 'Chosroes' who tore up the letter from God's Messenger (because Muhammed had written his name before that of the Emperor); however, he did that only after having read the entire letter and got to know the contents. So with Bilqîs: if she had not

---

[1] This refers to the Koranic recitation on Solomon, and the Queen of Sheba, whose Arabic name is *Bilqîs*: When Solomon reviewed the army of birds the Hoopoe bird brought him news from Sheba: 'There I found a woman reigning over men, who is provided with an abundance of things and hath a large throne. I saw that she and her people worshipped the sun besides God; and Satan hath beautified their works in their eyes, and hath turned them aside from the way of truth, wherefore they are not rightly directed, and they do not adore God who bringeth light to the secrets of heaven and earth, and knoweth whatever you conceal and whatever you manifest; God, beside whom there is no Divinity, Lord of the large throne. – Solomon said: We shall see whether thou hast spoken the truth, or whether thou art a liar. Go with this my letter, and deliver it to them and stand on one side, thou wilt see what their answer will be. (The Hoopoe bird having acquitted his mission, the Queen) said to the heads of her kingdom: O nobles, an honourable letter hath been delivered unto me: Verily it is from Solomon, and it is: In the name of God, the Clement, the Merciful, rise not up against me; but come and surrender yourselves unto me (to the will of God). . . .' (Koran XXVII, 23–31).

accepted (the grace) that was destined for her, respect of the author would not have prevented her from rejecting the letter, whether his name had been mentioned before or after the Name of God.

(At the beginning of the letter) Solomon mentioned the two Divine Mercies; the unconditional Mercy that corresponds to the Name of *ar-rahmân*, and the conditioned Mercy which corresponds to the name of *ar-rahîm*.[2] According to the first of these Names, God dispenses His Clemency without restriction (to all creatures); according to the second, He imposes it Himself as a duty (towards those who deserve it). Now this duty flows equally from His unconditioned Compassion, so that the sense of the Name *ar-rahîm* is contained in the Name *ar-rahmân*. For 'God prescribed Mercy to Himself',[3] destining it to His adorer in reward for the works that He mentioned (in the Holy writings) and from which the adorer acquired a right over God; who, He, made a law to be merciful towards the author of these works. But whosoever amongst the servants of God possesses this state (which guarantees him the Divine Mercy) knows thereby who is really the author of his works. For one divides the works (of adoration) in relation to the eight 'organs' of man (which are: the hands, the feet, the eyes, the ears, the tongue, the heart, the stomach, and the sex); but God makes it known to us (by the word often mentioned) that He is Himself the 'One' (*al-huwiyah*) of each of these 'organs'; then, God alone is author of all these acts; it is only the form which belongs to the servant himself, the Divine 'One' being principially inherent in him that is to say in his 'name' (which is his 'personal form') – for God is the essence of everything that is manifested and which is called creature. It is in this sense that one can attribute the Names 'the Exterior' (*az-zâhir*) and 'the Last' (*al-âkhir*) (Names which are, moreover Divine Attributes) to the servant; the second of these Names belong to him, moreover, because the servant comes from non-existence to existence. According to this same significance, the Names 'the Interior' (*al-bâtin*) and 'the First' (*al-awwal*) come back to God, because it is on Him that depend both the manifestation and the acts of the servant. So, when thou seest a creature, thou contemplatest the First and the Last, the Exterior and the Interior.

[2] These two Names are derived from *ar-rahmah*: the Merciful.

[3] (Koran VI: 12) *Katab-Allâhu 'alâ nafsihi-r-rahmah.* – This verse may also be translated as follows: 'God hath prescribed unto Himself Mercy' which means that Mercy, which is the 'beatific' aspect of Divine Infinity, has no other object but God.

This knowledge was by no means hidden from Solomon; on the contrary, for it belonged to a 'kingdom which belonged to no other' after him,[4] that is to say that nobody after him would manifest it in the sensible order. Muhammed received all that Solomon received, but he did not manifest it. It is thus that God had given *'Ifrit*[5] into his power, who had come in the night to harm him; but when he wanted to capture him and to tie him to one of the columns of the mosque until morning, so that the children of Medina could play with him, he remembered the prayer of Solomon, (who had prayed to God that He should accord to him a kingdom of which nobody after him should dispose) and found himself thereby prevented from manifesting his power as Solomon had manifested it. Now Solomon speaks of 'a kingdom' without generalizing, from which one learns that it is about a particular kingdom. However we know that he shares each part of this kingdom with others (Prophets and Saints), from which one will deduce that his privilege consists in the fact that he possessed this kingdom in its entirety. On the other hand it follows from the story of Afrit that only the exterior manifestation of this kingdom was the conclusive privilege of Solomon. To tell the truth, what really belonged to him was at the same time the synthesis and the exterior manifestation (of the kingdom in question). If the Prophet, in his telling of the encounter with Afrit, had not said: 'and God delivered him into my power', one could have believed that God reminded him of Solomon's prayer in the very intention of letting him know that he would not have the power to keep Afrit; but since he said: 'and God delivered him into my power', we know that he received the power with which to dispose, and only afterwards he remembered the prayer of Solomon and respected the privileged. So then, that which no creature after Solomon will dispose of, is the manifestation of this (cosmic) kingdom in all its entirety.

In all this we have before us only the two Divine Mercies that Solomon expressed by the two Names, which, in Arabic, are *ar-rahmân* and *ar-rahîm*, God conditioned the Mercy which He imposed on Himself as law and spread the other beyond all limit, according to His Word: 'My Mercy embraces everything',[6] that is to say that it embraces even the Divine Names – I mean the essential relations, for He showed

---

[4] (Koran XXXVIII, 34) . . . Solomon commanded genii, winds and animals.
[5] *'ifrit*: name of a category of mischievous genii.
[6] Koran VII, 155.

Himself merciful towards them in manifesting us; we are the fruit of Divine unconditional generosity towards the Divine Names (which demand creation as their logical complement) just as the dominical relations (which demand the servant as the object). Then, God prescribes His Mercy to Himself (or: for Himself) in manifesting us to ourselves; He makes us know our 'Being' (*huwiyah*), so that we should know that He destined His Mercy only to Himself, so that it never goes outside of Him; – and towards whom, then, apart from Him, would He be merciful, since there is only Him? Although one may certainly distinguish the degree of dignity (to receive His Mercy), since creatures have more or less knowledge, although the Essence be one. In fact, this hierarchical order of creatures in knowledge is analogous to that which exists between the Knowledge and the Divine Will, that is to say that it is reduced to the hierarchy of the Divine Qualities: the Will is inferior, in its connection with its objects, to Knowledge (on which it depends), as it is, on the other hand, superior in its relations to Power. Similarly, Divine Hearing and Vision, as all the Divine Names, constitute a hierarchy to which corresponds that of the manifested, so that one can say; this one is wiser than that one, although the Essence be one. In the same way that each of the Divine Names to which one attributes a dignity superior to that of the others, implies thereby the significance of all the others, each creature contains in itself the dignity of all that which is hierarchically subordinate. – (In fact) each particle of the world is the entire world, in the sense that it receives in itself all the different Essential Realities (*haqâïq*) which constitute the world. Thus our affirmation that such a one is inferior to such another in His knowledge, does not contradict the truth that the Divine Aseity (*al-huwiyah*) is the Essence at the same time of this one and that one, nor that this Essence is more perfect and more knowing in the second than it is in the first; in the same way that the Divine Names distinguish themselves, Names which are however nothing else than God: in His cognitive quality, God possesses a relationship (towards the possibilities) more universal than He possesses in His volitive quality or His quality of power, and nevertheless He is always identical to Himself and never becomes other than Him. Do not, then, know Him by only one side, O saintly man, and remain ignorant of Him on the other; do not affirm Him here, whilst denying Him there, unless thou dost affirm Him under the aspect in which He Himself affirms Himself, and thou dost deny Him equally under the aspect that He

Himself denies, according to the Koranic verse which synthesises the negation and affirmation towards God; 'Nothing is like Him, and it is He who Heareth and Seeth'.[7] In the first part of this verse, God denies (every quality with regard to Him), and in the second part He affirms (His Being) in respect of the quality which englobes all living beings gifted with hearing or with vision; but there exists nothing but living beings, although this truth be hidden in this world from the intelligence of many people, and it appears to everything only in the beyond, which is the abode of the living; as, for that matter is this world here, although its life (spread through everything) remains veiled for certain servants (of God), so that the degree of election and the hierarchy of the servants of God are manifested in those that know the Essential Realities of this world.

In the being in whom the intelligence is vaster, the Divine Principle is more apparent than in another in which the knowledge is more limited. Do not then, let thyself be confused by the difference of beings, and do not say that it is false to affirm that the creature is essentially God, when we have shown thee the hierarchy of the Divine Names, of which however, thou dost not doubt that they are God, and that their implicit significance is nothing else than their subject, that is to say, God.

But let us come back to Solomon: How could he have placed his name before that of God, as some affirm when he himself was one of those who owed his existence to the Divine Mercy? It was necessary for him to mention first the Compassionate, the Merciful, so that the connection of He who dispenses the Mercy to he who receives it be indicated with accuracy, for it is contrary to the order of the Realities that one gives precedence to that which must follow, or inversely.

The Wisdom of Bilqîs and her great science appear in the way in which she does not mention the messenger who conveyed the message to her; she acted thus so that her followers would remark that she had sources of information of which they were ignorant. That is a Divine disposition in the art of reigning. For if the way from which news reached the king remain unknown, the people of the government will be prudent and will not allow themselves to perform acts which would earn them the anger of their prince, if he grew to know of them. On the other hand, if they perceived by what intermediary news reached their king, they would try and corrupt this intermediary, so that they

7 Koran XLII, 9.

might do what they wished without the king's knowledge. The fact that she said simply : 'a letter has just been conveyed to me . . .' without naming the messenger, is then, an act of her policy which assured her the respect of her subjects and the dignitaries of the kingdom, and which justified her superiority over them.[8]

As for the superiority of the wise human over the wise among the genii (*al-jinn*),[9] it consists in the fact that the former knows the secrets of the transformations and the essential virtue of things. It is that which is expressed (in the Koran) by the lapse of time, (necessary, to one and to the other, to operate the transport of the throne of Bilqîs)[10] for 'the blinking of the eye' towards he who is looking is clearly more rapid than the gesture of rising from one's seat, since the 'movement' of the look in its perception of an object is more rapid than the displacement of a body; the 'movement' of a look is identical to the act of perceiving a thing, and this act does not depend on the distance which separates the spectator from his object : in the same moment which the eye opens, his glance already reaches the heaven of fixed stars. As for the time which is necessary for the 'blinking of the eye' towards the spectator, it is reduced simply to the cessation of vision. The act of a man rising from his seat is not of this nature, it has not this rapidity. Assaf ibn Barkhiyâ[11] was, then, superior to the genii by his manner of acting; at the same instant that Assaf ibn Barkhiyâ was speaking of the thing, his operation was accomplished and Solomon saw the throne of Bilqîs 'placed before him'; – (the Koran specifies it

[8] We may remark with regard to this that Ibn 'Arabi himself was adviser to several princes.

[9] The genii are subtle beings belonging to the same individual world as man. Whereas man was created 'of clay', genii were created 'of fire', that is to say that their vital environment is not the corporal state but the psychic state.

[10] This refers to the continuation of the story of Solomon and the Queen of Sheba, recounted in the Koran: '. . . . (Solomon said to his people): O lords, which of you will bring unto me the throne (of the Queen of Sheba) before they come and surrender themselves unto the Will (of God)? – It will be me, replied an Afrit from amongst the genii, I will bring it unto thee, before thou arise from thy place, for I am strong enough for that and faithful. – He who had the knowledge of the scriptures (said to Solomon): I will bring it unto thee, in the blinking of an eye. And when Solomon saw the throne placed before him, he said: This is a sign of the favour of my Lord. He tries me, to know whether I shall be grateful or whether I will be ungrateful. Whosoever is grateful is grateful to his own advantage; but whoever is ungrateful, God (may do without, for He) is Rich and Generous'. (Koran XXVII, 38-40)

[11] It is the name of Solomon's companion who operated the miraculous transfer of the throne; this name is not mentioned in the Koran.

in these words), so that one does not imagine that he saw the throne in its place (in the kingdom of Sheba) without it having been transferred. Now, there does not exist, in this world, instantaneous displacement, but the disappearance of the throne and its re-manifestation took place in a manner of which only he who knew it was conscious. It is found indicated in the Koranic word: 'They are illusioned by a new creation',[12] which means: not an instant goes by for them without their perceiving that which they see.[13] Since it is thus, the coincidence of the disparition of the throne from its former place with its re-apparition next to Solomon was due to the renewing of the creation 'by each breath – (nafas)'.[14] Nobody knows the power in question; for man does not notice spontaneously that which is not, and which is there again (lam yakun thumma kâna) at each 'breath'. And if I say 'again', I mean no temporal interval but a purely logical succession. In the 're-newing of creation at each breath', the instant of annihilation coincides with the instant of the manifestation of the similar one (mathal).[15] It is like the incessant renewing of accidents according to the Asharites.[16] The story of the removal of the throne of Bilqîs is one of the most perplexing (of the Koran) except for those who know the reality to which we allude. Assaf had no other merit than that of having trans-posed the renewal (incessant in the form of the throne) in the prox-imity of Solomon. The throne then was not transposed across space, and its dislocation does not abolish the spatial conditions, if one under-stands well what we have been saying.[17] (The transfer in question) was

[12] 'Are We then exhausted by the first creation? Surely, they are illusioned by a new creation' (Koran L, 14).

[13] The perception of the world is continuous in spite of its incessant renewal – See 'Introduction aux Doctrines Esoteriques de l'Islam' chapter 'Du Renouvel-lement de la Création'.

[14] Or: 'at each breath'. The breath of exhalation (nafas) is here the image of the expansive principle, the Divine Power which 'dilates' the worlds from their state of non-manifestation. In the chapter on Jesus, Ibn 'Arabi identifies 'The Breath of the Clement' (nafas ar-rahmân) to the Divine Mercy which 'dilates' (naffasa) the world. It is by that that the considerations on the throne of Bilqîs are connected to the initial subject of the chapter.

[15] The successive manifestation of one and the same archetype are similar or analogous amongst themselves. . . .; that is why the world of forms is called 'the world of similarities' ('alem al-amthâl).

[16] The theological school of the Asharites affirms an almost absolute dis-continuity of the world.

[17] The commentator al-Qashâni writes on the subject of this passage: 'The super-abundant flux of the One or the Breath of the Clement (nafas ar-rahmân), continually traverses existences, like the water of a river, renewing itself

operated by one of the companions of Solomon so that the latter would have honour in the eyes of Bilqîs and her suite, who were witnesses. The (profound) reason (of this miracle) lies in the fact that Solomon was a gift from God for David, according to the Word: 'And We gave to David, Solomon',[18] but, a gift is that which comes from the pure generosity of the giver, not that which one receives as recompense or because one has deserved it, and in this sense Solomon was himself 'the superabundant grace, the evident proof and the "coup tranchant".'[19]

As for the science of Solomon, God said of him (in the Koran) 'And we gave the understanding of this affair to Solomon';[20] – where the

----

ceaselessly. In the same way, the individuation of the One, received by the immutable essences (al-a'yân ath-thâbitah) contained in the eternal Knowledge, does not cease to renew itself, without discontinuity. Thus, it is possible that the primordial individuation of the Being be separated from its special determination and that it reproduces itself in another place, that is to say that the Essence manifests itself in another place after having disappeared as far as its manifestation goes in the first place, and that while remaining strictly identical in the Divine Knowledge and in the state of non-manifestation. It is this truth that Assaf ibn Barkhiyâ knew by Divine Grace. At the same time he was qualified to dispose of it by a 'supra formal' power (quwwatun malakûtiyah) . . . There is no temporal interval between the annihilation and the re-manifestation, so that one does not perceive an interruption between the two analogous and successive creations, and thus existence appears homogenous. . . In so far as man is a possibility of manifestation, but he does not see that which manifests him, he is pure absence ('udum); contrarily, in so far as he receives his being from the perpetual irradiation (tajallî) of the Essence, he is. The incessant revelation of the Divine Activities flowing from the Divine Names renews him after each annihilation, instantaneously, without perceptible temporal succession, but following a purely logical succession, for there is there but one permanent non-existence, which is that of pure possibility, and there is one permanent Being, the revelation of the Essence being one, and then the activities and the individuations succeeding each other with the breaths which flow from the Divine Names, since the individuals renew themselves at each present instant. . . .'

[18] Koran XXXVIII, 29.

[19] Arabic expressions.

[20] 'And remember also David and Solomon, when they pronounced judgement concerning a field, where the sheep of a certain family had caused damage. We were witnesses of their judgement. We gave the understanding thereof to Solomon, and to both of them the power of judgement and knowledge' (Koran XXI, 78–79). Here is the explanation of this passage: some sheep had done some damage in the fields of a farmer; the latter made the proprietor of the sheep appear before David, who decided that the farmer should take the sheep as compensation against the damage they had caused. Solomon, present at this judgement and then 11 years old, was of the opinion that it was more reasonable to give to the farmer the 'produce' only of the sheep, that is to say that the wool, the milk and the lambs of the sheep

judgement (of his father David) had failed, however, God gave 'to both the power of judgement (*hukm*) and a science ('*ilm*) . . .' That means that the science of David was science received (that is to say a reflected knowledge, become human), whereas the science of Solomon was the Divine Knowledge towards a certain thing, in this sense that Solomon identified himself directly to the Divine Judge, for he was the interpreter of God, in a state of perfect veracity. (The difference between the knowledge of Solomon and David) is analogous to that of a man who wants to know the Divine Judgement in a certain affair and who finds it by himself or by the grace of that which has been revealed to him by one of the prophets, and therefore has double merit, whereas another who has equally searched but is mistaken in his conclusion, has only the merit of his effort; the former has received a 'judgement', while the latter has only the 'science' (which renders him capable of searching) . . .

When Bilqîs perceived her throne, convinced that it was impossible to bring it from so far and in so short a time she said : 'it is as if it were itself';[21] in which she was right if one considers that which we have said about the incessant renewal of creation in similar forms; certainly it was it, and she spoke the truth in the sense where thou thyself art essentially identical, at the moment of thy renewal, to that which thou wert before.

The (spiritual) perfection of Solomon manifests itself also in the warning that he gave Bilqîs when he led her to the palace paved with crystal[22] which she took for a pond of water, so that she bared her legs so as not to wet her clothes. Solomon indicated to her from this that the apparition of the throne which she had just been shown was of the

---

would belong to him for a period of time sufficient to compensate his losses. David approved of the judgement of his son. (From M. Kasimirski: *Le Koran*).

[21] ' . . . Make this throne unrecognizable (said Solomon), we shall see whether she be rightly directed, or whether she be one of those who are not rightly directed. And when (the Queen) came it was said unto her: Is thy throne like this? She answered: It is as if it were the same (*ka-'annahu huwa*)' (Koran XXVII 41–42).

[22] ' . . . . It was said unto her: Enter this palace. And when she saw it, she imagined it to be a pool of water, and she uncovered her legs. Solomon said unto her: this is a palace paved with crystal. She said: my Lord, I have dealt unjustly with my own soul; I resign myself, together with Solomon unto God, the Lord of all the Universes. . . .' (Koran XXVII, 44–45).

same nature.[23] It is thus that Solomon awarded her full justice, making her understand in this manner that she was right in saying : 'it is as if it were itself'; upon which she said : 'Lord, I have wronged my soul, I submit with Solomon' – that is to say with the submission of Solomon – 'to God, the Master of the worlds'. In expressing herself thus Bilqîs did not make her submission depend on Solomon, but on the Master of the worlds, whereas Solomon was part of the worlds. The definition that she gives of her faith, then, does not differ from that which certain of Gods' messengers gave of theirs, contrarily to that of Pharaoh who did, when, on the point of drowning in the Red Sea, he referred to the Lord of Moses and of Aaron,[24] although the sense of his creed coincides in a certain aspect with that of Bilqîs, without being so direct. She was, then, wiser than Pharaoh in defining her attachment to God. It is true that Pharaoh was under the stress of the moment, when he said 'I believe in Him in whom the children of Israel believe'; saying that, he attached his faith to something in particular; but he did that because he had heard the (vanquished) magicians say, in affirming their faith in God; 'The Lord of Moses and of Aaron'.[25] As for the submission (islâm) of Bilqîs, she identified it with that of Solomon in the sense that she followed Solomon in all that was implied in the faith of the latter.

It is thus that we go along the straight Path (as-sirât al-mustaqîm) on which is found the Lord Himself, since He holds the 'forelock' in His Hand, so that we cannot be separated from Him.[26] We are then with Him implicitly, and He is with us sovereignly. For He says : 'God is with you wheresoever you are' (Koran LVII, 3) whereas we are with

[23] The commentator, an-Nâbulusi adds: 'that it to say, he made her understand that all that she had taken for real was but an illusion – or suggestion – just as the crystal of the palace had suggested water to her. . . .'

[24] 'And we caused the children of Israel to pass through the sea. Pharaoh, insolent and hostile, followed them with his army, until the moment when overcome by the waters, when he cried: 'I believe there is no other God but He in whom the children of Israel believe. I am of those who submit to Him. – Yes, at this time, but hitherto thou hast shown thyself rebellious, and thou wert of the transgressors' (Koran X, 90–91).

[25] This refers to the victory gained by Moses over the magicians of Pharaoh: ' . . . The magicians prostrated themselves, worshipping God, and saying: We believe in God, Lord of all the Universes, the Lord of Moses and Aaron.' (Koran VII, 117 sqq.)

[26] 'There is no live being, but He holdeth him by his forelock; verily my Lord is on the right way'. (Koran XI, 56).

Him because He caught hold of our 'lock'. In reality He is with Himself everywhere that He goes with us by His path, and in this sense, there is nobody in the world who is not on a straight path which is none other than the Path of the Lord, Exalted may He be! It is that which Bilqîs learnt from Solomon, and it is why she said: '(I submit myself with Solomon) to God, the Master of the worlds' without referring to any world in particular.

As for the cosmic domination which was the privilege of Solomon and which had been given to him by God as 'a kingdom of which nobody will dispose after him', it is a question of direct power of command (al-amr). For God said: 'We have rendered the wind to his service, so that it may blow to his order'.[27] His privilege then, did not consist in that fact that (the cosmic forces) were serviceable to him (as such), since God says with regard to each of us, without exception: 'He has rendered serviceable to you that which is in the heavens and on the earth and everything of His',[28] in the same way that He mentioned the winds, the stars, and other things which serve us not by our order but by the order of God. If, then, thou dost wish to reflect well on it, thou wilt find that the privilege of Solomon consists in the order (or command) acting directly, without his being in a state of concentration of his soul and without his projecting his spiritual will (himmah); we add this because we know that the bodies of this world obey the voluntary projection of the soul when this finds itself in a state of (spiritual) union, for we have made the experience in this spiritual path. He who looks for the power of Solomon (let him know, then), that which belongs to Solomon is only the action from the pure enunciation of the order, without spiritual aspiration nor concentration of the spirit. Learn also – and may God help us and thee, by a spirit emanating from Him – that when a certain gift befalls a servant (of God) whatever it may be, it will not be taken notice of in the beyond, that is to say, this gift will not be deducted from that which he shall receive there.

This is true for Solomon although he asked this gift of his Lord, and although, according to the intuition of men of this spiritual path, they accorded to him in advance that which He reserves for others (in the hereafter), and which, in consequence, He would deduct from their recompense if He wanted. But God had said to him: 'This is Our

[27] Koran XXI, 81.
[28] Koran XLV, 12.

gift'[29] without adding: for thee, or: for so and so, 'then dispense or keep it without counting'; from whence we know by intuition inherent to this spiritual way, that Solomon had asked for this gift by the order of His Lord, for if the request is made by obedience to the Divine Order, the one who requests receives full recompense, that is to say for having asked: as for the Creator (*al-bârî*), He bestows the request, if He wishes, or does not bestow it, the servant having in any case accomplished that which was demanded of him by the order of his Lord, since he addressed Him the desired prayer. On the other hand, if the servant addressed his request on his own initiative, without having received the order from the Lord, the gift, if He bestows it on him, will be deducted from his recompense in the hereafter. This law is applied to everything that one asks of God, May He be Exalted! In this sense, God said to His Prophet Muhammed: 'say: my Lord, augment my knowledge!' The Prophet obeyed this order of his Lord, and asked so much that his knowledge be increased, that each time one gave him milk, he interpreted it as signifying knowledge. It is thus moreover that he interpreted a dream in which he received a bowl of milk from which he passed what was superfluous to Omar ibn al-Khattâb; when his companions questioned him: 'and for what dost thou take it?' he replied: 'for knowledge'. In the same way, when God took him (at the time of the 'noctural voyage'), the Angel presented him with milk, and a vase full of wine,[30] and he drank the milk, upon which the Angel said to him: 'thou hast chosen the true Primordial Nature (*al-fitrah*); God will safeguard for thee thy community'. The milk is always the apparent form of knowledge, whatever may be the state of existence where it appears; to tell the truth, it *is* knowledge manifesting itself in the form of milk, just as Gabriel showed himself to Mary in the form of a harmonious man. When the Prophet said: 'men sleep, and when they die, they waken', he meant by that, that all that a man had perceived during his terrestrial life corresponds to the

---

[29] Koran XXXVIII, 38.

[30] According to another version of this same tradition, the Angel presented to the Prophet three bowls: one of milk, another of wine, and a third of water. These different drinks correspond to three spiritual tendencies; milk symbolizes the intellectual essence of the soul, so knowledge, or wisdom; wine represents love and spiritual drunkenness; and water represents the receptive purity of the soul; that is why the Angel said to the Prophet: 'If thou hadst chosen the wine, thy community would have strayed, and if thou hadst chosen water, it would have been dispersed'.

visions of someone who sleeps, so that everything demands interpretation. – In truth, the universe is imagination, and it is God according to His Essential Reality. He who understands that, has grasped the secrets of the spiritual path. – In this way, when one brought milk to the Prophet, he said: 'Oh God, bless us in this and give us more!' because he saw it as the apparent form of knowledge, and because God has ordered him to ask for the augmentation of his knowledge. And when one brought him something other than milk, he used to say 'Oh God, bless us in this and feed us by that which is better!'

If God gives something to somebody by virtue of a prayer enjoined by a Divine Order, this gift will not be deducted from those that one is to receive in the abode of the hereafter. On the other hand if He gives something to someone by virtue of a prayer which has not been enjoined by a Divine Order, so that the Order of God is not (necessarily) implied, God will compensate this gift, if He wishes, or will not compensate it, if He wishes. Hope, then, particularly, that God does not count His gifts of knowledge, since His order to the Prophet – on Him Benediction and Peace! – to request the augmentation of his knowledge is at the same time an order addressed to all his community. Does He not say: 'you have in the Messenger of God a perfect model'?[31] What model could be better than that one, if one understands it through God (that is to say through a Divine Knowledge).

If we exposed to thee the spiritual state of Solomon in all its plenitude, thou wouldst be struck with terror. The majority of the wise men of this spiritual way are ignorant of the true state of Solomon and his rank; the reality is not that which they suppose.

[31] Koran XXXIII, 21.

From the Sublime Wisdom
(al-hikmat al-'uluwiyah)
in the Word of Moses

ACCORDING to the spiritual significance (*hikmah*) the killing of the male children (of the Israelites, whose murder was ordered by Pharaoh) for the purpose of destroying the prophet (whose birth had been predicted),[1] took place so that the life of each child killed in this intention flowed into Moses; for it was in supposing that one of them was Moses that the children were killed; now, there is no ignorance (in the cosmic order) so that the life (that is to say the vital spirit)[2] of each of these victims necessarily had to return to Moses. It was life that was pure, primordial, not having been soiled by egotistic desires. Moses was then (by his psychic constitution) the sum of the lives of those who had been killed in the intention of destroying him. From then on, everything that was prefigured in the psychic predisposition of each child killed, was to be found in Moses, all of which represented an exceptional Divine favour that nobody before him had received.[3]

(Conforming to his psychical constitution) the wisdoms of Moses[4] are numerous. If God wills, I will expose some in this chapter, bit by

[1] According to certain traditions, the Egyptian astrologers had predicted to Pharaoh the birth of an Israelite prophet who would destroy him.

[2] The vital spirit (*ar-rûh*) is the intermediary between the immortal soul and the physical organism. It is dissolved generally after death; in certain conditions, it can transfer itself entirely or partially on a living man, like a collection of forces carrying the imprint of the soul of the deceased; it is that which takes place in the succession of hierarchies of the lamas called *Tulku*. Al-Qashani adds that Pharaoh, who wanted to prevent the Divine prediction by killing the male children of the Isrealites, favoured in this way the manifestation of the prophet, who was to be as the synthesis of the souls of his people. One may remark the reciprocal relation between sacrifice and salvational descent.

[3] According to the Zohar, Moses was not only the representative of the people of Israel, but the people itself in the eyes of God.

[4] That is to say the Divine Wisdom, which manifested itself in the words, the acts, and even in the destiny of Moses.

[96]

bit, as the Divine Command inspires me. Now, the first thing of this order that was taught me, is that which I have just mentioned.

Moses, then, was born as a synthesis of many vital spirits, which were as many active forces; for the young act on the adult. Dost thou not see how the little child influences the adult by the attractive power which is innate in him, so that the adult puts aside his dignity to amuse the child, to make him laugh, and he puts himself at the same level as the childish intelligence. It is that he obeys unconsciously the power of the fascination of the child, who thus obliges him to occupy himself with him, to protect him, and to procure for him that which he needs, and to console him too, so that he feels no anguish. All that is part of the influence that the young exercises on the adult; the cause is the power of the state, for the young one is more directly attached to his Lord, because of his primordiality, whereas the adult is more remote. Now, he who is nearer to God makes himself served by he who is further away, like the angels closest to God are served by the others. The Messenger of God had a habit of exposing his bare head to the rain, when it started to fall, and he said of the rain, that it came fresh from his Lord. Consider then, this knowledge that the Prophet had of God (manifested by this gesture); is there anything more luminous, more sublime and clearer? It is thus that the rain fascinated the most noble of men by its proximity towards his Lord; it was sent as if it was a celestial messenger which brought him Divine inspiration. It attracted the Prophet spontaneously, by virtue of its essential nature, so that he had to offer himself to it in order to receive that which it brought him of Divinity; for he would not have exposed himself to the rain if it had not transmitted a Divine benefit. There is the mediatorial (risâlah) function of water, from which God 'made every living thing'[5] – understand that well!

As for the wisdom implied in the fact that Moses was put in an ark and abandoned to the Nile, we will say that the ark (at-tâbût) corresponds to his human receptacle (an-nâsût) and the Nile to the knowledge that he had to assimilate by the mediation of this body, that is to say by means of thought and faculties of sensation and imagination, faculties which would not be able to transmit something to the human soul without previous existence of this body composed of elements. Only when the soul arrives in the body and disposes of it by Divine Order, and governs it, is it endowed with corresponding faculties, which

[5] Koran XXI, 31.

permit it to realize that which God wishes it to realize by the government of His ark where lives the Peace (*as-sakînah*) of the Lord.[6] It is thus that Moses was exposed in his ark on the Nile, so that he should realize by these faculties the respective domains of knowledge. God taught him by this that if the spirit is the King (of the human organism), it rules however only through it, that is to say by the intermediary of the faculties attached to this human receptacle (*an-nâsût*) of which the symbol is the ark.[7] In the same way, God rules the world only through the world itself, or by its (qualitative) 'form'. He rules it through Himself, according to the law which makes the existence of the generated depend on that of the generator, the ending on their ends, the conditioned on their conditions, the effects on their causes, the conclusions on their proofs, and everything that is true on the truths which define it. For all that (each and every one of these terms) make part of the world,[8] so that God (co-ordinating these complementaries) governs the world by the world; we have added: 'or by the form of the world'; by that we meant the essential form of the world, meaning the Divine Names and the transcendent qualities of God. In fact, we have not learnt a Divine Name of which we did not find the significance and the spirit in the world; so that in this respect God only governs the world through the 'form' of the world. It is for that, that (the Prophet) said on the subject of the creation of Adam, who is the prototype synthesising all the categories of the Divine Presence – the Essence (*adh-dhât*), the Qualities (*as-sîfât*) and the Activities (*al-af'âl*), – that 'God created Adam in His form'. But, His 'form' is none other than the Divine Presence Itself, so that God manifested in this noble 'resumé' which is the Perfect Man (or Universal Man; *al-insân al-kâmil*) all the Divine Names and the Essential Realities (*al-haqâïq*) of every-

---

[6] *As-sakînah* corresponds to the Hebrew *ha shekkîna*, indicating the Presence of God in the ark of the alliance. It is the body which is the support of the 'real Presence' and not the mental.

[7] So that, there too, the manifestation of the Essential Reality depends formally on its support: the Spirit (*ar-rûh*) rules the body by the intermediary of the mental and the faculties of sensation and action on which existence, like differentiated faculties, depends on that of the body.

[8] God then is neither a truth nor a cause in the cosmological sense of the term, nor an end. Or, if God is the cause of the world, in the sense that essentially He contains it, the cosmic causality will be no more than a symbol of this principial relationship, consequently the cosmic causality does not contain its effect in all respects; thus for example, the soul has need of the body to manifest certain of its virtualities.

thing that exists outside of him, in the macrocosm, in a 'detailed' manner. He made of the Perfect Man the spirit of the world and subjected to him the high and the low[9] because of the perfection (or universality : *kamâl*) of his 'form'. In the same way that there is 'no thing' in the world which does not exalt God by his praise,[10] there is nothing in this world 'which does not serve this Man' because of the essence of his 'form' : 'God has rendered serviceable to you that which is in heaven and on the earth, everything from Him';[11] everything that the earth contains is subject to Man. This is known by he who knows, meaning by the Universal Man, and ignored by those who are ignorant, meaning the animal man.[12]

According to appearances, the fact that Moses was put in the ark and abandoned to the Nile, signified his loss; in reality it was by that, that he was saved and that he lived, in the same way that the soul is revived by knowledge after its death in ignorance, according to the Koranic Word : '. . . or he who was dead', in ignorance, 'and whom We have revived, by knowledge, 'in giving him a light with which he walks among men,' – this light being the Divine direction, 'is he like the one who, in the parable, finds himself in the shadows' of error 'never emerging from them',[13] – the state of ignorance being in itself indefinite, without a term of ending.

The Divine guidance consists in the fact that man be brought to perplexity (*al-hayrah*) (in the face of suprarational Reality), so that he may know that existence is entirely perplexity (meaning oscillation between two Divine aspects apparently contradictory); but, perplexity is instability (in the sense of non-inertia) and movement, and movement is life, so that there is neither inertia nor death, but pure existence, without absence.

Such also is the nature of water, which communicates life to the earth and provokes movement, according to the Koranic Word : 'And thou seest the desert of earth, and when We cause water to descend on it, it trembles, and conceives and produces' – or brings forth – 'all sorts

---

[9] The world of active spirits and that of receptive materials.

[10] Koran XVII, 46.

[11] Koran XXII, 64.

[12] This is to say that this sovereignty of man cannot be known except in the pure Spirit, essentially identical to the prototype of the universe, whereas the psychic and sensible faculties do not grasp it.

[13] Koran VI, 122.

of couples in beauty',[14] that is to say that it brings forth only that which conforms to its own nature which, itself, is subject to duality, which is polarity.[15] In the same way, the Divine Being assumes the multiplicity (of aspects) and Names, which it designates as such or such, in the view of the world, which presupposes from its nature the multiple essences of the Names which it affirms therein. Inversely, the multiplicity of the world is unity, in respect of its essence. In the same way that the Hylé is multiple by virtue of the forms which appear in it, and of which it is the substantial support, God appears as multiple by virtue of the forms of His own revelation, so that He is the 'place of revelation' (majlâ) where the forms of the world reveal themselves the one to the other, at the same time remaining essentially one.[16] – Consider then, the beauty of this Divine teaching, of which God accords the comprehension to those that He chooses from amongst His servants.

When Pharaoh's family found Moses in the Nile, close to a tree, Pharaoh called him *Mûsâ-mû* meaning in Egyptian 'water' and *sa*, 'tree', – because the ark had been stopped against a tree in the flood of the river. First of all Pharaoh wanted to kill him, but his wife opposed him, speaking from Divine inspiration, since she had been created for spiritual perfection, according to the Word of the Prophet who said that she and Mary attained the perfection of the perfect ones amongst men.[17] She said, then, to Pharaoh on the subject of Moses: 'He will be a consolation for me and for thee',[18] and in fact, it was by him that she was consoled by receiving spiritual perfection, as we have just said. On the other hand, he was a consolation for Pharaoh too, because of the faith that God gave him (before he was drowned in the Red Sea), so that God seized the spirit of Pharaoh in a purified state, without blemish, since He seized him in his (newly acquired) faith, before he could soil it by a sin; for the submission to God effaces all sin which precedes it. So, He made of him a sign of His help liberally accorded to whosoever He wishes (according to the Koranic Word:

[14] Koran XXII, 5.

[15] The polarity is the proper character of Universal Nature of which earth is the symbol.

[16] The substantial unity, passive, of Nature or of the Hylé is the inverse image of the Essential Unity.

[17] 'Amongst men, many have attained perfection (al-kamâl), but amongst women only Assiyah, the wife of Pharaoh, and Mary. . . .'

[18] Koran, XXVIII, 9.

'so that thou wilt be a sign for those who will live after thee')[19] and that nobody despairs of the Divine Mercy for: 'none despaireth of the Spirit of God, but the misbelievers'.[20] If Pharaoh had been of those who despaired, he would not suddenly have submitted to God.[21] So, Moses was, as the wife of Pharaoh said: 'a consolation for me and for thee; do not kill him, possibly he could be of use to us'.[22] It is exactly that which happened, for God was good to them because of Moses, although they had no idea that he was the prophet who was to destroy the reign of Pharaoh and his family.

When God protected him thus from Pharaoh, the heart of his mother was relieved of the sorrow which had oppressed her. Then, God prevented the child from accepting a wet nurse until he received the breast of his mother, who then fed him, and by this God rendered her joy perfect.[23] This case is analogous to the knowledge of the different sacred ways (sharâ'i), according to the Divine Word: 'To each of you we have given a path (shir 'aten) and a direction (minhâjâ)';[24] this latter term means when one separates the minhâ and jâ'[25] the provenance of a being; now this corresponds in nutrition to the material milk, just as a plant is nourished by its root. (Conforming to this

[19] Koran X, 91.

[20] Koran XII, 87.

[21] 'And we led the children of Israel through the sea. Pharaoh, insolent and hostile, followed them with his army. But when the sea menaced to engulf him, he said: I believe that there is no other God than He in whom the children of Israel believe, I submit to Him. Now thou believest it when before thou wert rebellious and transgressing. This day we will raise thy body from the bottom of the sea, that thou mayest be a sign unto those who shall live after thee. Verily a great number of people are negligent of our signs'. (Koran X, 89–91).

[22] Koran XXVIII, 10.

[23] 'The heart of the mother of Moses became oppressed with grief; and she almost divulged his origin; (she would have done so) had We not strengthened her heart so that she became a believer. And she said unto her sister: Follow the child. She watched him from a distance without her being noticed.

We forbade him the breasts of the foreign nurses who were provided for him until the moment (when, the mother's sister, arriving) said to the Pharaoh's family: would you like me to direct you to a house where they will nurse him for you and look after him well?

Thus We restored him to his mother, that her sad eyes might be consoled, and that she might no longer be afflicted; and that she might know that the promises of God are infallible. But the greater part of mankind know it not'. (Koran XXVIII, 9–12).

[24] Koran V, 52.

[25] Minhâ = from her; jâ' = has come.

principle, which has it that a being should be nourished only by its root), a thing may be illicit according to a certain sacred way, and licit according to another, – I mean according to appearances, for, in reality it is not a question of one and the same thing, in this case as in the other, since the Divine Order (that is to say Existence) is made of continual renewal of creation, without any repetition. But, this Divine divergence of sacred paths is symbolized, in the story of Moses, by his aversion against the wet nurses.

The real mother of a child is she who gives him her milk and not only she who gave birth to him, for the latter carried the child like something which had been confided to her, who grows in her and is nourished by the blood of her womb without the will of the mother being incurred, nor her generosity, for the embryo feeds itself only of blood which would render the mother ill and kill her, if the child did not feed from it and the blood could not escape from her. It is, then, the embryo which is a blessing for the mother, because it nourishes itself from the blood of the womb and thus protects her from the sickness that the retention of it would cause her. Such is not the case of the mother who feeds, for in giving her milk she wishes to conserve the life of the child. But, God destined as wet nurse to Moses, the mother who bore him, so that no woman other than his mother should have a right over him, and also that she should be consoled in rearing him, and seeing him grow at her breast.

Thus, God saved Moses from the anguish of the ark; and because God gave him knowledge, he pierced the shadows of his (physical) nature without, however, emerging from it. He was tested 'by many ordeals',[26] that is to say that God instructed him under many appearances, so that he could acquire patience in the Divine ordeals. The first of the ordeals was the murder of the Egyptian,[27] an act which he committed by Divine impulsion and with the approbation of God deep inside him, without however, his perceiving it; nevertheless he felt no affliction in his soul for having killed the Egyptian, although he him-

[26] Koran XX, 41.

[27] 'One day he went into the city, without being noticed, and he found two men fighting: the one was of his own nation the other was his enemy. The man of his nation begged his assistance against the one who was of the enemy nation. Moses struck him with his fist, and slew him; but, recovering from his temper, he said: this is the work of Satan; for he is an enemy who obviously leads us astray. Lord, verily I have acted wrongly towards myself, forgive me. So God forgave him; for He is Indulgent and Merciful'. (Koran XXVIII, 14–15).

self was not acquitted until he had received a Divine revelation on the subject. For all prophets are interiorly preserved from sin without their being conscious of it, even before they are warned by inspiration. It is for that reason that Al-Khidr showed him the putting to death of the boy, an action for which Moses reproached him, without remembering his murder of the Egyptian, upon which Al-Khidr said to him: 'I have not done it on my own initiative', recalling thus to Moses the state in which he, the latter, found himself when he did not yet know that he was essentially preserved from all action contrary to the Divine Order.[28]

He showed him also the perforation of the boat, apparently made to destroy the people, but which has, however, the hidden sense of saving them from the hand of a 'violent man'. He showed this to him as an analogy to the ark which hid Moses when he was thrown into the Nile; according to appearances, this act was equally to destroy him, but according to the hidden sense, it was to save him. Again his mother had done that from fear of the 'violent man', who is Pharaoh, so that he would not cruelly kill the child. And she watched him, re-assured by Divine inspiration that she did not realize, finding in herself the certitude that she would nourish him; but, fearing for him, she threw him in the Nile, as if she were saying to herself (as in the proverb): 'that which the eye does not see, does not afflict the heart', and so that she would not fear for him as if she had to witness (his death); but the thought that God would give him back to her perhaps (imposed itself on her) because of her confidence in God, and it was with this thought that she lived, her hope compensating her fear and her despair. When she had the inspiration to expose him on the Nile, she said to herself perhaps it is this one that is the prophet by whom

[28] This refers to the Koranic text on the meeting of Moses with Al-Khidr, the mysterious person to whom God affirms that He gave the 'science' which is 'close to Me' (*ladduni*). The name of Al-Khidr, which means 'the Green', is not mentioned in the Koran; it has been conserved by oral tradition. For Islamic esotericism, this person plays the same role as Elijah in Judaic esotericism. Moses wanted to follow Al-Khidr, so that the latter could teach him his knowledge of the 'right path'. But Al-Khidr insinuates that Moses will never have enough patience with him; all the same he accepts his company, on condition that Moses questions none of his actions, before he has said something about them; '. . . . So they both travelled until they embarked on a boat, and he made a hole therein. Moses said: Hast thou made a hole therein that those who are on board might drown? Verily thou hast done a strange thing! – He answered: Did I not tell thee that thou wouldst have no patience with me? Moses said:

Pharaoh and the Egyptians will be destroyed and she lived with this imagination, which was in itself knowledge.[29]

Then, when they were looking for Moses (after he had killed the Egyptian) he 'left the town, fleeing through fear' (of punishment)[30] according to appearances, but in truth he fled through love of salvation, for the impulse of movement is always love, although the observer may be confused by the appearance of secondary causes. But there does not exist such or such a (true) cause of movement, for the principle of movement is the passage of the world from its state of nonmanifestation, where it is in repose (in so far as pure possibility), to the manifestation. From then one says that the (Divine) Order (al-amr) is movement disengaging itself from repose. Now, this movement which is the very existence of the world is the movement of love, as the Word of the Prophet indicates (pronounced in the Name of God): 'I was a hidden treasure. I loved to be known and I created the world';[31] if there had not been this Divine Love the world would not have been

Rebuke me not, because I did forget, but impose not on me too difficult an order. They proceeded, until they met a youth that he slew. Moses said to him: Hast thou slain an innocent person, without his having killed another? There thou hast committed an action hard to bear. He answered: Did I not tell thee that thou wouldst have not patience with me? Moses said: If I ask thee concerning anything hereafter, suffer me not to accompany thee; I have offered thee my excuse. They travelled, until they came to the inhabitants of a certain city. They asked the inhabitants to give them food but they were refused hospitality. And they found therein a wall, which was ready to fall down; and he set it upright. Whereupon Moses said unto him: If thou wouldst thou might have received a reward for it. He answered him: This shall be our separation, I will give thee the explanation of that which thou hadst not the patience to wait for. The vessel belonged to certain poor men, who did business in the sea. I wanted to render it unserviceable, because there was a king behind them, who took every sound ship by force. As to the youth, his parents were true believers, and we feared lest he oppressed them by perversity and misbelief. We desired that their Lord might give them a more righteous child in exchange for him, and one more worthy of mercy. As to the wall it belonged to two young orphans in the city, and under it was a treasure hidden which belonged to them. Their father was a saintly man, and thy Lord was pleased that they should attain their full age, and take forth their treasure, through the mercy of thy Lord. I did not do that of my own will. Such is the interpretation of that which thou couldst not bear with patience'. (Koran XVIII, 64–82).

[29] 'Here is what We inspired to the mother of Moses: Give him suck, and if thou fearest for him, cast him into the Nile and fear not; do not be afflicted, for We will restore him unto theee one day and We will appoint him one of Our apostles'. (Koran XXVIII, 6).

[30] Koran XXVIII, 21.

[31] hadîth qudsî.

manifested. The movement of the world from non-existence to existence is then (in reality) the movement of love manifesting itself. On
the other hand the 'world' also loves to contemplate itself as existing,
just as if it contemplated itself in its state of principial immobility.
Under which ever face one considers it, the movement of the world
from its state of permanent non-existence towards its existence would
be a movement of love, from the Divine side as well as the worldly
side.

For the Essence loves perfection (al-kamâl); but, the knowledge that
God has of Himself in so far as He is independent of all worlds, refers
only to Himself; so that knowledge be perfect in all degrees, it is necessary that knowledge of the ephemeral, knowledge which results precisely from these determinations, – meaning the determinations of the
world in so far as they exist – is realized equally. The Divine perfection
(or the Infinity) expresses itself then, in that it manifests relative knowledge as well as eternal knowledge, so that the Divine dignity of Knowledge be perfect under the one and the other aspect (although relative
knowledge adds nothing to Absolute Knowledge).

In the same manner the Being perfects itself. For the Being (al-
wujûd) is in one way eternal and in another way non-eternal or to
become. The eternal Being is the Being of God in Himself; the non-
eternal being is the Divine Being (reflecting Himself) in the 'forms' of
the immutable world (that is to say in the archetypes); it is that which
one means by 'become' (or happening; hudûth) because the Being is
manifested there from one part to the other. He manifests Himself,
then, to Himself in the forms of the world, so that the Being be perfect
(in every respect although the relative can add nothing to the eternal).[32]

The movement of the world, then, is born of the love of perfection
(or of infinity). Dost thou not see that (God) relieved (naffasa, a word
which contains an allusion to the Breath of Compassion; nafas ar-
rahmân) the Divine Names from their state (of contraction, where they
found themselves) before the manifestation of their effects in this substance called world? He loves the repose (or relaxation; ar-râhah), and
he attains it only through formal existence, neither more nor less. From
this it results that movement is motivated by love, and that there is no
movement in the cosmos which is not a movement of love.

There are some wise men who know this, and others who are de-

---

[32] The same idea, a Sufi master of our days explained in these terms: 'God
is so great that He can even assume limits without His being limited by them'.

luded by the existence of secondary causes, more apparent at the moment given, and of which the soul is more conscious. Thus, fear was more conscious within the soul of Moses, because of the killing of the Egyptian, but this fear implied love of his own salvation and so he fled 'through fear', which means that he fled because he wanted to escape from Pharaoh and from the punishment that he would make him suffer; he himself only mentioned (in his dialogue with Pharaoh)[33] the immediate cause (of his flight from Egypt), that of which he was conscious at the given moment, like the man is immediately conscious of his own body, whereas the love of salvation was implicit, like the spirit is immanent in the body.

The prophets use a concrete language because they address themselves to the collectivity and they trust in the comprehension of the wise one who will hear them. If they talk figuratively, it is because of the ordinary people and because they know the degree of intuition of those who really know. It is thus that the Prophet said, in speaking of generosity, that he gave nothing to certain people who were more dear to him than others, for fear that God would throw them into the eternal fire. He expressed himself thus for the feeble minded who is a slave to avidity and natural inclinations.

In the same way, all that the prophets brought of sciences is clothed in forms which are accessible to the most ordinary intellectual capacities, so that he who does not go to the heart of things stops at this clothing and takes it for that which is the most beautiful, whereas the man of subtle comprehension, the diver who fishes the pearls of Wisdom, knows how to indicate for what reason such or such a Divine Truth is clothed in terrestrial form; he evaluates the robe and the material of which it is made, and knows by that, all that it covers, attaining thus to a science which remains inaccessible to those who do not have knowledge of this order.

Since the prophets, their messengers and their heirs know that there are in the world and in their own communities men who possess this intuition, they rely in their demonstrations on a concrete language equally accessible to the elite as to the common man, so that the man

[33] 'Pharaoh said to Moses: Have we not brought thee up amongst us when a child; hast thou not dwelt amongst us for several years of thy life? Then thou hast done the deed which thou knowest; thou art an ungrateful person. He replied: Yes, I did this deed; but then I was one of those who erred. And I fled from amongst you through fear. Then God bestowed on me the power of judgement and appointed me one of His apostles'. (Koran XXVI, 17–20).

of the elite can gain at the same time that which the ordinary man gains and more, according to the measure in which the term of 'chosen' (*khass*) is applied really to him and distinguishes him from the blind man; and it is by that (by this intuitive understanding) that the wise are distinguished, the ones from the others. Such, then, is the meaning of the expression of Moses: 'and I fled from amongst you through fear' instead of saying: 'I fled from amongst you through love of salvation'.

He arrived then at Median, there met the two girls and for them drew water from the well, without asking from them a salary.[34] Then he 'withdrew to the shade', that is to say to the Divine shadow, and said: 'Oh my Lord, I am poor with regard to the blessings Thou bestowest on me'; he attributed, then, to God alone the essence of the good that he did and qualified himself as poor (*faqîr*) towards God. It was for that that Al-Khidr reconstructed before him the crumbling wall without asking a salary for his work, for which Moses reprimanded him, until Khidr reminded him of his action of drawing water without asking for reward, and other things too, of which there is no mention in the Koran; so that the Messenger of God – May God bless him and give him Peace! – regretted that Moses did not keep quiet and did not remain with Al-Khidr, so that God could tell him more of their actions.

By that one can see the state to which Moses was elevated without his being conscious of it; for had he been conscious, he would not have denied the same thing in Al-Khidr, of whom even God had witnessed before Moses that he was pure and just; in spite of that, Moses forgot the Divine justification as well as the condition under which he had been permitted to follow Al-Khidr, which happened by Divine Mercy towards us, in case we should forget the commandment of God. If Moses had been conscious (of the spiritual state which had made him act in such a way towards the two maidens of Median), Al-Khidr would not have said to him: '(God has given me a knowledge) which thou

[34] 'When he was journeying towards Median, he said: Peradventure, my Lord will direct me in the right way. When he arrived at the water of Median, he found there a company of men, who were watering their flocks. Beside them he noticed two women who kept off their flocks at a distance. He asked them: What do you need? They answered: We cannot water our flocks until the shepherds shall have gone away; for our father is an old man stricken in years. So Moses watered their sheep for them; and afterwards retired to the shade saying: My Lord! I am poor compared to the good with which Thou gifted me'. (Koran XXVIII, 21–24).

hast not learnt', that is to say, I possess a knowledge of which you have no intuition, in the same way that thou dost possess a knowledge which I do not. So he was right. As for his decision to separate from Moses, God Himself said 'That which the messenger brings you, grasp, and that which he forbids you, flee from',[35] and by this Word God obliges the wise ones who know the extent of the function of the Divine Messenger. But, Al-Khidr knew that Moses was a messenger of God; so he paid attention to whatever emanated from him, so as not to lack respect towards the messenger of God. Moses had said to him: 'If I ask thee once more about something, then thou wilt no longer keep me company', and by that he prevented him from staying with him; when Moses questioned him for the third time, Al-Khidr said to him: 'This is our separation', and Moses did not answer him: 'no', and he did not ask him to stay, for he knew the extent of his own dignity of messenger, which had made him forbid him to accompany him further; he was silent, then, and they separated. Consider the perfection of these two men in their knowledge and in their tact with regard to the Divine Reality, in the same way as the impartiality of Al-Khidr – Peace be on him! – when he said to Moses: 'I possess a science which God has taught me and which thou dost not know; and thou dost possess a science which God has taught thee and which I do not know.'[36] This word like balm on the wound that he had inflicted on him in saying '. . . and how wilt thou have the patience with regard to (the things) that thy science does not englobe';[37] saying that, he knew that Moses had received the dignity of messenger of God, whereas he himself had not that function. The same (distinction in sciences) appears, in the breast of the Muhammedan community, in the recital of the fertilization of the palm, where the Prophet says (to his companions): 'You are wiser than I in the things of your world'. Now, there is no doubt that the knowledge of a thing is worth more than the ignorance with regard to it; so God praises Himself in affirming His conscience; the Prophet realized, then, that his companions were more knowledgable in the useful things of this world, since he had not learnt them, because it was a question of empiric science and he had not been free to acquire it, occupied as he was by Divine inspiration.

[35] Koran LIX, 7.
[36] According to a word of the Prophet, cited by al-Bukhâri and others.
[37] Koran XVIII, 67.

I have just shown thee an act of supreme politeness, which may be very useful to thee, if thou take it to heart.

As for the word of Moses (addressed to Pharaoh)[38] '. . . and God has invested me with the power of judgement' (hukm), it indicates the function of representative (khalîfah) of God on earth, whereas the following; 'and He made of me one of the number of the envoys' indicates the Divine mission (ar-risâlah); for every envoy is not God's representative on earth; the representative of God judges by the sword he destitutes from power and he institutes; whereas the envoy only transmits the mission with which he has been charged; if he fights for his mission and defends it by the sword, he is the representative of God on earth and envoy of God at the same time. In the same way that every prophet is not an envoy,[39] every envoy is not God's representative on earth, disposing of rule and of the power of temporal judgement.[40]

As for the question of Pharaoh on the Divine Quiddity (mâhiyah).[41] ('What is (ma) the Lord of the worlds?'),[42] it was not asked in ignorance, but in the intention of proving Moses, who declared himself the envoy of the Lord. For Pharaoh knew very well what should be the state of knowledge of an envoy, so he wanted to test Moses by this question, to see if he was sincere. On the other hand it is because of those who were present that he posed an imaginary question, so as to show them what he had presentiment of in posing his question, without their perceiving (his ruse); for if Moses replied in the way that he who has knowledge of Reality should reply, Pharaoh would demonstrate, in favour of his own dignity, that Moses had not replied suitably to his question, so that the (courtiers) who were present should believe, in the narrowness of their views, that Pharaoh was wiser than Moses. Thus, when Moses gave him the answer suitable to such a question, (he replied: 'The Lord of the Heavens and of the Earth and of that which is between the two, if you have the certitude')[43] but which did not appear to correspond to that which had been asked – and Pharaoh

---

[38] Koran XXVI, 20.

[39] The prophecy is characterized by Divine inspiration, but only the Divine mission (al-risâlah) implies the promulgation of a new sacred law.

[40] One will remember the Word of Christ. . . . 'My reign is not of this world' (St. John XVIII, 36).

[41] From ma: 'that'. Latin: quid. al-mâhiyah is therefore the nature of a thing.

[42] Koran XXVI, 22.

[43] Koran XXVI, 23.

knew very well that he would answer in this manner – Pharaoh could say to his retinue : 'In truth your envoy' – he who has been sent to you – '. . . is possessed',[44] that is to say that his intelligence is veiled, he is not capable of seeing that on which I have questioned him, as it is moreover not suitable that one should know what it is about (or : that he should know it).

The question (of Pharaoh) was valid as such, for the question on the Quiddity refers to the Reality (*haqîqah*) of that on which one informs oneself; but, there is no doubt that the object of the question is in itself real. As for those who say that the definition (replying to the question : 'quid est?') should be composed of genus and species, they are right for all that may be associated to something else (and which is therefore included in a category); but that which passes beyond the genus is not necessarily devoid of reality in itself, for this reality may not belong to any other thing (as in the case for the Reality of God). The question, then, was valid according to the usage of those who know, the wise ones and the reasonable men; in the same way, one could not reply otherwise than did Moses.

Therein lies a great secret : Moses replied by demonstrating the action, when he had been questioned on the essential definition of that which was in question; so he made from the relation of God towards the forms which are manifested by Him – or in Him – the essential definition (of God), as if he said, in replying to he who wanted to know what is the Lord of the world : 'It is He in whom are manifested the forms of the world, from their supreme degree – Heaven – to their lowest degree – the earth –, if you have the certainty'; or 'He who manifests Himself by the forms of the world' etc. When Pharaoh then said to his court that Moses was possessed – according to the sense which we have explained – the latter added another demonstration, to let Pharaoh know his degree of Divine Knowledge; for Moses knew that Pharaoh was knowledgeable in these things; so he said 'The Lord of the East and the West' mentioning from whence (the sun) appeared and that by which it is hidden, for God is at once the Apparent (*az-zâhir*) and the Hidden (*al-bâtin*) – 'and of that which is between the two' – God knowing everything 'if you reason'[45] that is to say, if you hold to discursive reason, which delineates things.

The first reply was addressed then, to those who possess the certitude

[44] Koran XXVI, 26.
[45] Koran XXVI, 27.

(*yaqîn*) meaning intuition (*kashf*) and the identification of the Being (*al-wujûd*) for he says: 'if you have the certitude' – you, men of intuition and identification, for I let you know that of which you already have a direct knowledge in your conscience and by your state of being; but if you are not of this category of men, then I answer you by my second reply, since you are tied to reasoning (*'aql*) and to formal limitations, so that you shut in the Truth in discursive arguments. In this way Moses manifested the two faces (of knowledge) so that Pharaoh should recognise his superiority and his sincerity; for Moses knew quite well that Pharaoh knew all that, since the latter had questioned him on the Quiddity (of God) and Moses realized that Pharaoh did not pose this question according to the custom of philosophers who expect a definition; it is for that moreover, that he answered him; for if he had understood Pharaoh's question otherwise, his response would have been at fault. Moses having affirmed that the reality to which the question referred was the essence of the world, Pharaoh in his turn used this manner of expressing himself, without the people perceiving it, he said to Moses: 'In truth, if thou takest another than I for Divinity we will imprison thee';[46] now, in the word prison (*sijn*) (composed of the letters *sîn*, *jîm* and *nûn*) the *sîn* makes up part of the accessory letters (so that the subtle significance of the word resides in the group *jîm-nûn*, which contains the idea 'to hide', to 'occult' or 'to veil'); so he made him understand that he was going to confuse him as if he said 'By that which thou hast answered me (that is that the Divine Reality is the essence of the world) thou dost authorize me to say as much to thee (in affirming that this same Divine Essence is present in my person); and if thou dost answer me in hidden language; I ignore, O Pharaoh, thy pretention towards me, since the Essence is one (and it is present in me as in thee) how then dost thou separate it? – I would reply: I do not separate the Essence; I separate only the degree of manifestation of the Essence; certainly the Essence is indivisible, inseparable as such, but the degree of its actual manifestation in myself, is that of power over thee, O Moses; I am thee by the essence but I am other than thee by dignity'. Consequently, Moses understood this thought of Pharaoh's and he gave him his due on his own plane and let him understand that Pharaoh would not have the power (to confuse him). The dignity (which Pharaoh attributed to himself), is proved by the power and the ability to act on the other, for in this assembly (where

[46] Koran XXVI, 28.

[111]

Moses and Pharaoh were) the Divine Reality manifesting itself exterior-
ly in the dignity of Pharaoh dominated the dignity which clothed
Moses. From this fact, Moses made a barrier of hostility of Pharaoh
and said to him: 'And if I produce something evident'.[47] Then
Pharaoh could not avoid saying: 'Produce it then if thou are sincere',[48] so as not to appear unjust in the eyes of those of feeble mind
in his own retinue. For they already had doubts about him; they were
the sect of people that Pharaoh held under his domination inspiring
them with frivolity, and who obeyed him because they were 'corrupt
people',[49] that is to say because they were not within the framework
of those of sane reason, who necessarily would reject a pretention like
that of Pharaoh (proclaiming himself God) according to the letter; for
reason stops at a certain limit, which is surpassed only by intuition and
the (contemplative) certitude. It is for that, that Moses addressed himself in his answers to those who possessed the certitude of the one hand,
and to those who had reasoning, on the other.

'Moses threw his staff (*assâ*)' this being the apparent form of that
by which Pharaoh had 'disobeyed' ('*assâ*) Moses in rejecting his request
– 'and there it became an evident dragon',[50] that is to say a visible
serpent; disobedience, which is vice, transformed itself thus into obedience, which is virtue, according to the Divine Word 'God changes their
vices into virtues';[51] that is to say according to the (Divine) judgement.
The judgement appeared here as diverse essences in one unique substance, for it is a question at once of a staff and a serpent or 'evident
dragon'. As a serpent, it swallowed other serpents, and as a staff, the
staffs (of the magicians). It is thus that the proof of Moses vanquished
the proofs of Pharaoh in the forms of sticks, serpents and ropes. When
the magicians saw this, they knew the degree of Moses' knowledge,
for that which they saw surpassed the limits of man; it was only
possible for man, by virtue of a knowledge which distinguished between the reality and the imagination or illusion. From then on they
believed in the 'Lord of the worlds, the Lord of Moses and Aaron',[52]
that is to say the Lord towards whom Moses and Aaron called men;

[47] Koran XXVI, 29.
[48] Koran XXVI, 30.
[49] 'Pharaoh inspired his people with light behaviour, and they obeyed him,
for they were corrupted' (Koran XLIII, 54).
[50] Koran XXVI, 31.
[51] Koran XXV, 70.
[52] Koran XXV, 46–47.

[112]

(and they expressed it thus) because of the people who well knew that Moses did not call them towards Pharaoh. However, as Pharaoh had the function of authority, as he was the lord of his time, and he represented God with the sword, though at the same time transgressing against the sacred Law, he said: 'I am your supreme Lord'[53] that is to say although you may all be lords in one respect, I am the supreme Lord because of the apparent authority which has been given to me. The magicians, knowing what he said was truth, did not contradict, but confirmed it saying: 'thou dost rule only this earthly world, so decide what thou dost want the reign is thine' (Koran XX, 75); – therein is the sense of the words: 'I am your supreme Lord'. For, if (the supreme Lord) is none other than the Divine Essence, the individual form that assumed this essence was that of Pharaoh. Thence, the action of cutting off the hands and feet and of crucifying[54] was accomplished by the Divine Essence clothed in a vain form so as to realize the degrees of being[55] which could be realized only by this act. The linking of causes could not be abolished, determined as it is by immutable essences (al-a'yan ath-thâbitah) for these manifest themselves in existence according only to the 'forms' which they imply in their state of permanence; 'There is no change for the Words of God';[56] but, the Words of God are none other than the essences of living things; they are eternal in their state of immutability, and they are in the future (hudûth) in so far as they appear in existence.[57]

As for the Divine Word: 'And when they see Our punishment, their faith will be of no use unto them. Such is the Divine custom which will perpetrate itself amongst His servants'[58] and excepting for the people of Jonah,[59] that does not signify that the faith of those who saw the punishment will not serve them (in the hereafter), excepting for the

[53] Koran LXXIX, 24.

[54] 'Pharaoh said: I will have your hands and your feet cut off alternately, I will have you all crucified'. (Koran XXVI, 49).

[55] That which the condemned magicians were to realize after their death.

[56] Koran X, 65.

[57] Here we omit an example that the author mentions as a proof of this thought, an example which is uniquely founded on 'arabisms'.

[58] Koran XL, 85.

[59] 'Those against whom the word of Thy Lord has been pronounced shall not believe, although there comes unto them every kind of sign, until they see the grievous punishment. If it were otherwise, a town which had believed, would have found in that its salvation. Except for the people of Jonas: when they believed, We delivered them of the punishment of shame in this world, and We let them subsist until a certain term'. (Koran X, 96–98).

people of Jonah, but that their belated faith could not prevent punishment seizing them on this earth. For this reason Pharaoh was destroyed despite his faith, be it that it came at the moment when he was certain of his imminent destruction, be it that he thought he could save himself; but, the immediate situation, at the moment that he testified his faith, proves that he was not certain of his death, since he saw the believers walking on the dry path which had opened in the sea when struck by the staff of Moses. Pharaoh, then, was not certain of his destruction until the moment when it happened. He believed in that which the children of Israel believed. ('I believe that there is no Divinity other than that in which the children of Israel believe')[60] while still having the certitude of his salvation; so that in which he believed happened, although it was in a different manner from that which he had wished, for God saved him from infernal punishment in his soul and saved his corpse (from the waves), as it is said in the Koran: 'That day, as far as thy body goes, We will save thee, so that thou mayest be a sign for those who will live after thee',[61] for if the corporal form had disappeared, his people could have said that he had been hidden from them (by his ascension to heaven). His dead body, then, reappeared and was recognised by his people. It is thus that salvation reaches into the soul and the body.

As for he who is struck by the Divine decree of punishment in the hereafter, he does not believe even if every Divine sign is given him; ('Those against whom the word of thy Lord has been pronounced do not believe, even if every sign has been given to them, until they see the painful punishment'),[62] that is to say until they experience it. Pharaoh was not of this category; it is that which becomes evident from the text revealed. We will say again referring ourselves in this to God, that the general belief in the condemnation of Pharaoh rests on no sacred text. As for his people, they suffered another law, but this is not the place to talk of it.

Know that God does not take the soul of a man without the latter believing, that is to say without Divine messages; I mean by that those who are conscious of death; and for this reason, one abhors sudden death and the killing of the unconscious. As for sudden death it is defined by that which strikes a man after a single respiratory phase,

[60] Koran X, 89.
[61] Koran X, 92.
[62] Koran X, 96.

the breath exhaled not being inhaled. In this condition, the man is not aware. In the same way the killing of the unconscious consists in the striking of the nape of the neck from behind, without his seeing it, so that his soul is seized in the state in which it was at that very instant, in faith or in unbelief, upon which the Prophet said: 'man is summoned (to the last judgement) in the state in which he died', in the same way that his soul is taken in the state it was at the moment of death. On the other hand, he who is conscious of death is necessarily witness (of the Divine Reality which manifests itself to him in the instant of death); he believes, then, that which he witnesses, and his soul will be taken in this state; for it is an existential letter (harf) which is not connected to time except by the logical linking of the states;[63] his soul, then, is taken such as it is. For this reason one makes a distinction between the infidel who is conscious of his imminent death, and the infidel killed in unconsciousness or dead of a sudden death, according to the sense that we have described above.

God talking to Moses from the burning bush appeared to him in the ignited form because Moses had been looking for fire;[64] and God appeared to him as the object of his desire so that he was directed towards Him and did not turn back; for if God had revealed Himself to him under some other form, not desired by him, he would have turned away because of his concentration on this particular aim. But, if Moses had drawn away from God, his action would have recoiled upon him, and God in his turn would have drawn away from him. But Moses was chosen and close to God, and if God causes one to approach Him, He reveals himself to him as the object of his desire, without his knowing.

As the fire of Moses, which he saw through the eye of his need,
And who is the Divinity that he did not recognize.

---

[63] Just as time, in a sentence, does not condition the words as such, but only their occasional linking.

[64] 'Hast thou heard tell of the story of Moses? When he saw a fire he said unto his family: Stay here, I have just perceived some fire. Peradventure I may bring you a brand thereof, or may find a direction in our way by aid of the fire. And when he was come near unto it, a voice called out to him saying: O Moses! Verily I am thy Lord: put off thy sandals, thou art in the sacred valley of Tuwâ . . .' (Koran XX, 8 sqq.)

From the Wisdom of the Singularity
(al-hikmat al-fardiyah)
in the Word of Muhammed

(THE essence of) his wisdom is singularity (or 'incomparability'), because he was the individual who was the most perfect of the human
species.[1] It is for that, that the creative act (al-amr) started with him
(in so far as permanent prototype) and ended with him; for, on the
one hand he was 'prophet', when Adam was still 'between water and
clay'[2] and, on the other, he was in his terrestrial existence, the 'seal'
(khâtim) of all the prophets.[3]

The first singular number, from which all the others are derived, is
the ternary.[4] Now, Muhammed was the first symbol of his Lord, for

---

[1] This does not signify, in the perspective of Ibn 'Arabi, that Jesus was less
perfect than Muhammed; only the perfection of the former is situated, in a
way, beyond the series of human beings, Christ not having a human father. The
Prophet, on the other hand, was entirely man from the paternal as well as the
maternal side. It goes without saying that these considerations contain no
'ingerence' in the sense of Christian dogma, which affirms the perfect humanity
of Christ.

[2] Word of the Prophet.

[3] He is called 'Seal of the Prophets' because there are no more prophets after
him, until the end of the present cycle of humanity. The role of 'seal' implies
a synthesis of that which precedes it: the message of Muhammed confirms and
resumes that of the preceding prophets. By his spiritual reality, hence, 'interior', Muhammed is necessarily identified to the Eternal Word; on the other
hand, his cyclic role 'terminates' the terrestrial manifestation of the Word. This
polarity of the two principial and temporal aspects of the Prophet is situated
in another cosmic 'dimension' from that of the two 'descents' of Christ, of
which the first announced the end of the present cycle, whereas the second will
open the future cycle.

[4] 'Fard' means at once 'singular' and 'odd'. The first odd number is three,
unity being not a number but the principle itself in the sense of numbers. The
first metaphysical ternary is that of the one who Knows (al-'âqil), of the Known
(al-ma'qûl) and of Knowledge (al-'aql), the first cosmic ternary that of the
Kalame (active essence), the Guarded Table (the passive substance) and of the
Universal Book (their communal product).

he had received the 'universal words', which are the contents of the names which God taught to Adam; so he had the triple nature of the symbol, this being (in reality), the symbol of himself.[5] It is because the Essential Reality (*haqîqah*) of Muhammed contains the primordial singularity – manifest in all that is naturally triple – that he says, in speaking of love, source of all existence : 'Three things of your world, amongst all that it contains in triple, have been made worthy for me of love', that is to say, women, perfume, and prayer, where he found the 'freshness of his eyes'.[6]

He mentioned women in the first place and prayer in the last, because woman is part of man through her origin, which manifested her,[7] and man must first know of his own soul before being able to know his Lord; for his knowledge of the Lord is like the fruit of his knowledge of himself, from whence the Word of the Prophet : 'He who knows himself, knows his Lord' (*man 'arafa nafsahu faqad 'arafa rabbahu*). From this one may deduce, either that God cannot be known and that one will be unable to reach Him – which is perfectly valid – or that God may be known. It is necessary that thou knowest, first that thou dost not know thyself, and then thou knowest thyself and that, in consequence, thou knowest thy Lord.

Muhammed was the most evident symbol of his Lord in the same way that each part of the Universe (of which Muhammed represents the qualitative synthesis) is the symbol of its origin, which is its Lord. Women 'were made worthy of love' to him in the sense that he leant towards them with the affection of the whole for its parts. It is this which expresses, in its intimate reality and from the Divine point of view, the Word of God on the creation of man; 'And when I had unfolded his form, and I had blown into him of My Spirit'.[8] Again, God speaks of His intense desire to encounter man, for He says to David on the subject of those who desire Him : 'Oh David, it is I who desire them even more intensely'.[9] That which He desires is a partic-

---

[5] So that the symbol contains an essence, an apparent form and that which attaches this to that. The logical significance of the symbol coincides with its ontological essence.

[6] Arabic metaphor which means 'consolation'.

[7] It is not in the essence that woman is part of man, the essence being independent from the polarity of sexes, but in her cosmic determination, which is hierarchically inferior to that of man.

[8] Koran XV, 29.

[9] According to a Word of the Prophet.

ular encounter, of which it is said in the *hadith* on the Antichrist:
'None of you will see your Lord before he dies'. It is necessary, then,
that the desire to encounter God, amongst those who have this quality,
be really intense. As for the desire of God towards those who are close
to Him, – and who moreover, He sees already, as He sees all beings,
but those whom He wants to be able to see Him equally, which their
state prevents – as for this desire, we were saying, it is analogous in the
sense of the Divine Word: 'We will test them until We know'[10] and
yet, God knows all. It is that He desires to manifest this particular
(Divine) quality which can be manifested only at the death (of those
who love Him). By this quality He puts to the test the desire they have
for Him, as He says in the *hadith* on the Divine hesitation, words
which refer equally to those of whom we are speaking here: 'In no
other thing that I do, do I hesitate so much, as in taking the soul of
My beloved servant, who has a horror of death; and I have a horror
of hurting him; however he has to meet Me'. In expressing Himself
thus, God consoles His servant; He does not say: 'and however he has
to die', so as not to afflict him with the idea of death; but since man
can only encounter God after his death – according to the Prophet:
'None of you will see your Lord before he dies' – He says: 'And however he has to meet Me'. But, God lets us know that He breathed into
man His Spirit, so that it is Himself that He desires; for has He not
created man in His 'form', which means that he issues from His Spirit.

From the fact that man in his natural constitution, is composed of
four elements that one also calls 'humours' in respect of their (organic)
manifestation in the body, the Divine Breath, kindling by contrast with
the humidity contained in the human body, conferred to the human
spirit its igneous nature.[11] For this reason God addressed Himself to
Moses in the guise of fire, after having provoked in him a desire to find
it.[12] If human constitution participated directly to Universal Nature
(which englobes also the angels), the spirit blown into it would be
(pure) light. On the other hand, if God symbolised (His act of Creation) by the blowing, it is that He was alluding to the Breath of Compassion (*nafas ar-rahmân,* that is to say the merciful expansion of the
possibilities of manifestation starting from their latent state in the

---

[10] Koran XLVII, 33.

[11] It is that which constitutes the difference between the transcendent spirit
and the vital spirit, the igneous quality being co-extensive to the individual life,
subtle and physical.

[12] Koran XX, 8–10.

Source).[13] By the Divine Breath, the essential determination of man was made manifest; and because of the predisposed receptacle, the Spirit appeared, not as Light (*nûr*) but as fire (*nâr*). The Divine Breath, then, is inherent in that by which man is man (in the sense of his primordial human quality). Of this (primordial) nature (of man) God caused there to be derived a second 'person', created in his form, and called it woman. As soon as this latter appeared in the form of man (or as an image of his essential 'form'), he leant towards her, because a being loves himself, and she turned towards him, as to the country of her birth.

Thus women 'were rendered worthy of love' in the same way that God loves that which He created 'in His form', so that He ordered the angels of light, in all their power and the height of their rank and nature, to prostrate themselves before him.[14] From there comes the (intimate) relationship (between God and man). It is the form (in the purely qualitative sense of the term) which constitutes the highest, the most brilliant and the most perfect of relationships, for it is in a way the 'duplicate' of the Divine Existence, in the same way that, by her existence, woman duplicates men and makes of him one of the poles of a couple. There is then a ternary: God, man and woman; man reaches out towards his Lord, which is his origin, as woman reaches out towards man.

God 'rendered to him women worthy of love'; in the same way that He loves that which He created 'in His form' (Divine) Love has for its object only that which issues from the loving being; and the love of the Prophet springs only from that which he had himself come from, that is to say God; it is because of that, that he said; 'they were made for me worthy of love' and not that he loved them through himself alone; for his love was attached to his Lord, from whence he received his 'form' – even his love for his wife, whom he loved by virtue of the love of God for him, by identification with the Divine Love.

When man loves woman, he desires union, that is to say the most complete union that can be possible in love; and in the form composed of elements, there exists no union more intense than the conjugal act. From this voluptuousness spreads through every part of the body and

[13] The Clement (*ar-rahmân*) sitteth on His Throne' (Koran XX, 4); now the Throne symbolises the integral manifestation; it is, then, under His aspect of Blessed Mercy (*ar-rahmâniyah*) that God 'deploys' universal manifestation. On the theory of the Divine Breath see '*Introduction aux Doctrines Esoteriques de l'Islam*' p. 69.

[14] Koran II, 30–34.

for the same reason sacred law prescribes total ablution (of the body after the conjugal act), the purification having to be total, just as the extinction of the man in the woman has been total after the voluptuous rapture (of the sexual union). For God is jealous of His servant, He does not tolerate that the latter may enjoy anything but Him. So He purifies him (by the rite prescribed) so that he returns, in his vision, towards Him in whom he is extinguished in Reality – since there is nothing else but that.

When man contemplates God in woman, his contemplation rests on that which is passive; if he contemplates Him in himself, seeing that woman comes from man, he contemplates Him in that which is active; and when he contemplates Him alone, without the presence of any form whatsoever issued from him, his contemplation corresponds to a state of passivity with regard to God, without intermediary. Consequently his contemplation of God in woman is the most perfect, for it is then God, in so far as He is at once active and passive that he contemplates, whereas in the purely interior contemplation, he contemplates Him only in a passive way. So the Prophet – Benediction and Peace be on him – was to love women because of the perfect contemplation of God in them. One would never be able to contemplate God directly in absence of all (sensible or spiritual) support, for God, in His Absolute Essence, is independent of worlds.[15] But, as the (Divine) Reality is inaccessible in respect (of the Essence), and there is contemplation (shahâdah) only in a substance, the contemplation of God in women is the most intense and the most perfect; and the union which is the most intense (in the sensible order, which serves as support for this contemplation) is the conjugal act.

This act corresponds to the projection of the Divine Will on that which He 'created in His form', at the very moment when He created him, there to know Himself, and He deployed it, and fashioned it harmoniously and blew into it His Spirit, which is none other than Himself, so well that the exterior (of primordial man) is creature, and his interior is God. This being so, God endowed man with the faculty of disposing of this temple (the human body), the same as God 'disposes of order', from heaven which is the supreme degree of existence

---

[15] The contemplation (shahâdah or mushâhadah) implies a certain polarity of subject and object; polarity that only the Essential Knowledge can surpass; but in this case, there no longer exists either individual subject or objective world.

– 'unto the earth'[16] – which is that which is the most base, the element of the earth occupying the lowest place in the hierarchy of elements.

Talking of women, the Prophet calls them *an-nisâ,* a plural which has no corresponding singular;[17] for he said : 'Three things in your world were made for me worthy of love, women (*an-nisâ*)' etc and not : 'woman' (*al-mar'âh*), thus alluding to the fact that women occupy an ontological position behind his own; the root of the word *nisâ,* in fact, means to come later, to be last. But, the Prophet loved women precisely because of their ontological rank, because they were like the passive receptacle of his act, and because they were situated in relation to him as the Universal Nature (*al-tabî 'ah*) in relation to God, it is certainly in Universal Nature that God causes the forms of the world to blossom by the projection of His Will and by the Divine Command (or the Act : *al amr*), which manifests itself as the sexual act in the world of forms constituted by the elements, like spiritual will (*al-himmah*) in the world of the spirits of light, and as logical conclusion[18] in the discursive order, the whole thing being but an act of love of the primordial ternary reflecting itself in each and all its aspects.

He who loves women in this manner, loves them by Divine Love; but he who loves them only by virtue of natural attraction, deprives himself of the inherent knowledge of this contemplation. The sexual act will be for him a form without spirit; of course, the spirit always remains immanent in the form as such, only, it stays imperceptible to he who approaches his wife – or some other woman – only for voluptuousness, without really knowing the object of his desire. This man is as ignorant with regard to himself, as a stranger would be to whom he had never made himself known.

People know well that I am in love;
Only, they do not know with whom . . .

This applies well to he who only loves for voluptuousness, that is to say he who loves the support of voluptuousness, the woman, but remains unconscious in the spiritual sense of that which is really in question. If he knew it, he would know by virtue of what he enjoyed

[16] Koran XXXII, 4.
[17] According to the commentator an-Nâbulusî, the collective form always expresses the passivity.
[18] That is to say as the 'coupling' of the premises, which engender the conclusion.

[121]

it, and who (really) enjoys this voluptuousness;[19] then, he would be (spiritually) perfect.[20]

In the same way that woman (in her natural condition, not in her intelligent essence) occupies an inferior degree to that of man[21] – confirming the Koranic Word: 'As for men, they precede (in their legal dignity) women by one degree';[22] the being created 'in the form of God' occupies a degree hierarchically inferior to He who created him 'in His form', in spite of the identity of the form of the One and the other. It is precisely by this degree, that the Creator is distinguished from His Creation, that God is 'independent of worlds', and the first agent; for the second agent is the 'form', although it obviously does not have the role of an autonomous principal. It is thus that the essential determinations (al-ayân) distinguish themselves one from the other by virtue of their (ontological) ranks, and it is in the same manner as that, that all who know (God) grant to every real thing its degree of reality; so Muhammed – Benediction and Peace be on him – was to love women through Divine Love. As for God, He 'gives to each thing its own nature'[23] so its own reality : which comes back to saying that He gives to each thing, only that which is essentially due to it, by that which in itself it represents (as possibility).

The Prophet mentioned women in the first place, because they represent the passive principle and Universal Nature (which is the universal plastic principle) precedes whatever manifests itself, from it by (the action of) the 'form'. But, Universal Nature is none other, in reality, than the Breath of Mercy (an-nafas ar-rahmânî) in which are deployed the forms of the world, from the highest to the lowest, by the infusion (suryân) of the Divine Breath in the 'materia prima' (al-jawhar al-hayûlânî); it is that which has taken place for the world of (terrestrial and celestial) bodies; as for the infusion of the Divine Breath (in Total

---

[19] The Divine Reality being at the same time the veritable Subject and Object of all primordial acts.

[20] By the union, in his spiritual consciousness, of the primordial complements.

[21] In his Futûhât, Ibn 'Arabi specifies that woman is virtually capable of the same spiritual perfections as man, which is proved by the existence of women who are 'perfect like the mother of Christ, the wife of Pharaoh, and the daughter of the Prophet'; it is the cosmic condition of woman which is inferior to that of man; also women who are spiritually perfect are more rare than men who have reached this perfection.

[22] Koran II, 228.

[23] Koran XX, 52.

Nature) at the time of the manifestation of the spirits of light and the (general) conditions (of existence), that is of another order.[24]

In his sentence ('three things of your world'), the Prophet gave prevalence to the feminine over the masculine, insisting by that on the role of woman; for he says *thalâthun* for 'three', a word which is employed in Arabic only for feminine collectivity; however, of the three things enumerated (that is women, perfume and prayer) there is one which is masculine; perfume; and the Arabs always give prevalence to the masculine; for example they say 'les filles et le garçon sont presents' and not 'presentes', without regard to the numerical pre-eminence of the feminine element in the collective. Now, the Prophet was an expert in the Arabic language (so he was perfectly conscious of the employment of the term), and he wanted to allude to the spiritual significance of this love, with which he had been inspired without his having chosen it voluntarily; it is thus, moreover, that God 'taught' him that which 'he did not know previously'[25] and that the Divine favour towards him was immense. So he gave prevalence to the feminine over the masculine in expressing himself in this manner; and who then would know better than he the principial truths and would be more perspicacious with regard to the laws? In addition, he made the last of the three things mentioned, the pendant of the first by the feminine gender and inserted the male reality between the two, for he started by the mention of women and ended by that of prayer, the one and the other notions having the feminine gender; as for the perfume it is found mentioned between the two, by the analogy with the ontological situation of the Prophet himself; man finds himself (in fact) placed as an intermediary between the Essence (*dhât*) from which he emanates, and woman, who emanates from him; he is situated, then, between these two feminine entities, of which one, the Essence, is feminine by notion, and the other is really feminine, in the same way as women, in the sentence stated by the Prophet, are really feminine, whereas prayer is only verbally feminine; perfume is situated between the two, as Adam is situated between the Essence which manifests him, and Eve who manifests herself from him. Moreover, if thou preferest,

[24] The result of this is that for Ibn 'Arabi the Universal Nature (*tabî'at al-kull*) is analogous to that which the Hindus designate as Prakriti, whereas the 'materia prima' (*al-jawhar al-hayûlâni*) corresponds only to the plastic substance of the formal world, just as the Hellenistic cosmologists understand it.

[25] Koran XCVI, 4.

[123]

thou mayest replace 'Essence' by 'Quality' or by 'Power'; whatever may be the term that thou dost choose for the first entity, it will always be feminine, even if thou followest the custom of certain (cosmologists) who will make of God 'the cause' of the universe, for 'cause' is equally of feminine gender.[26]

As for the spiritual significance of perfume, that the Prophet mentioned after women, – because of the perfumes of existence[27] which are to be found in women, and which causes it to be said currently : the best scent is the embrace of the well-beloved, – this significance is the following : the Prophet was created as the adorer 'par excellence' (al-'abd) who never lifted his head to attribute to himself the Lordship[28] but never ceased to prostrate himself and to stand before God, in the state of (perfect) receptivity, until God drew from him that which He had created in him, and conferred on him the active function in the world of spiritual emanations (anfâs) which are the perfumes of existence (renewing themselves unceasingly from the archetypes). It is for that reason that perfume was rendered to him worthy of love and that he mentioned it after women.

By this order (going from women to perfume and prayer), the Prophet respected the ascending order of the Divine manifestations (which, from the relative point of view, proceeds from the indistinct potentiality of the passive substance towards the complete actualization of all the virtual contents), order to which the Koranic Word alludes : 'He who exalts by degrees, the Lord of the Throne . . .';[29] God is there called 'Lord of the Throne' because of His 'enthronement' (at the time of His integral manifestation) in His Name the Compassionate (ar-rahmân), according to the Word; 'The Compassionate is sitting on the Throne');[30] all that the Throne englobes is reached by the Divine

---

[26] Al-Qashâni draws attention to the fact that the male corresponds to the determination, whereas the feminine nature is relatively indeterminate, since it is related to the unformed receptive substance; it is this aspect of the feminine nature that the verbal symbolism transposes by inverse analogy to the principial Nature, of which the reality surpasses all determination or form.

[27] Literally: of 'existentiation' (takwin); it is a question of the 'exhalations' (anfâs) of the Divine Mercy which 'dilate' (naffasa) the possibilities susceptible of existence.

[28] According to the Word of the Prophet 'Say of me: the servant ('abd) of God and His Messenger, so that you do not fall into the exaggeration that the people manifest with regard to my brother Jesus'.

[29] Koran XL, 15.

[30] Koran XX, 4.

Mercy (*rahmah*), conforming to the Word (*hadîth qudsî*); 'My Mercy englobes all things', so the Throne englobes all things.[31] It is from the principle of this revelation of *rahman* on the Throne which englobes all (*ar-'arsh al-muhît*) that the Divine Mercy is spread to the interior of the earth, as we have already explained in this book and in our *Futûhât*.

Perfume is mentioned with respect to sexual union in the Koranic passage attesting the innocence of 'Aishah (the wife of the Prophet whom certain people had wrongly slandered). God says of this : 'Let impure women be with impure men, and the impure men with the impure women, and let pure women be with pure men, and pure men be with pure women; these are exempt from whatever (the slanderers) may say . . .' Koran XXIV, 26, (passage which may also be translated thus : 'Let malodorous women belong to malodorous men, and malo- dorous men to malodorous women; and let sweet smelling women be- long to sweet smelling men, and sweet smelling men to sweet smelling women . . .'; the pure, then, are described as exhaling a good odour (just as the word 'good' is called in the Koran *tayibah*, that is to say 'good' or 'sweet-smelling') because the word is essentially respiration as odour is essentially exhalation; the word, then, may be said to be good smelling or bad smelling following that which it manifests by its verbal content. In so much as the word (or the breath) is principially Divine in its essential reality, all enunciation is good (or good smelling); but as soon as one applies the distinction of good or bad,[32] it is either good (or good smelling) or bad (malodorous). It is thus that the Prophet said of garlic : 'It is a plant whose odour I detest', he did not say :

---

[31] The Throne (*al-'arsh*) 'englobes all things'; it symbolizes the universal manifestation taken in its total unfolding, which contains balance and harmony; it is the support of the glorious manifestation of God, of the Merciful Beatitude (*ar-rahmâniyah*). Although intemporal from the Divine point of view, the total unfolding of the cosmos presents itself relatively as its final accomplishment. The Divine Throne is 'above the waters' (Koran XI, 9), that is to say that it dominates the totality of cosmic potentialities or the ocean of the primordial substance; this recalls the Hindu and Buddhist symbol of the lotus which blossoms on the surface of the water and which is at once the image of the universe and the seat of the revealed Divinity. Essentially, the Throne is identi- fiable with the Universal Spirit. According to the Sufi point of view, everything, considered in its primordial nature, is the Throne of God. In particular it is the heart of the contemplative which identifies itself to the Throne, just as the lotus, according to the Buddhist–Hindu symbolism is identified with the heart.

[32] That is to say; as soon as one considers it in its distinctive particularity, which is either conforming, or contrary to the perfections of the Being.

'That I detest', for the essence of the thing itself is never detestable;[33] one detests a certain manifestation, this aversion, moreover, perhaps arising from a custom, from the non-affinity of natures, from an individual tendence, from a sacred law, from a lack of required perfection and from other factors again.

Since the Divine Order (al-amr) is divided into good and bad, as we have just established, the Prophet was endowed with the love of the good (or good odour) to the exclusivity of bad (or bad odour). The Prophet said of the angels who are offended by bad odours, that since man was created 'from clay and fermented mire'[34] that is to say putrified, angels detested *man* by nature. The scarab, on the other hand, cannot bear the perfume of the rose, although it is one of the best; but for the scarab, it is bad. In the same way, every man who has the temperament of the scarab, mentally and formally, cannot bear the truth when he hears it, but tastes on the contrary, vanity, according to the Koranic Words; 'those who believe in vanity but do not believe in God . . .'[35] and further on '. . . it is they who are the lost ones', who lose themselves, for he who does not distinguish good from bad (or the good odour from the bad) has no intelligence.

God inspired in the Prophet, love of only the good in everything, and there is, essentially, only good. Now, is it conceivable that there exists in the world a constitution which experiences only the good in everything and ignores the bad in it? We will say that this is not possible, for, in the principle itself, from which the world emanates, that is to say in God, we find denial and love; but, the bad is none other than that which one detests, and the good that which one loves;[36] the world is created 'in the form of God' (therefore according to love and to denial); as for man, he is created according to two forms (that of God and that of the world). There cannot exist, then, a constitution which perceives only one aspect of Reality; on the contrary there can certainly exist a constitution which distinguishes the good from the

[33] Because this essence comes from cosmic necessity, from a Platonical 'idea'.

[34] Koran XV, 26.

[35] Koran XXIX, 52.

[36] Ibn 'Arabi is thinking here of the sense that one gives 'in fact' to the word 'bad' and not of that which one should give it 'en principe'. It is all the same astonishing that Ibn 'Arabi does not express precisely this shade of meaning, or only expresses it implicitly in saying he who does not distinguish good from bad is devoid of intelligence. If the angels have an aversion for man, it is for an objective reason, the 'light' of which they are created being more conforming to the pure Being than to the 'black mud'.

bad (or the good smelling from the bad-smelling) at the same time knowing moreover that which is bad by its flavour is good in itself, disregarding the flavour. That this being be distracted, by his concentration on the good, from the sensation of bad, certainly, that exists; but as for saying that the bad could disappear from the world, that is to say the cosmos, that is something impossible. The Divine Mercy, it is true, manifests itself in the bad as in the good; (for there is no absolute bad, all badness shows then good aspects, even though they be minute); a bad being is good in himself (in the homogenity of the complete system that he represents), and it is to him that the good appears as bad; there exists nothing good which is not bad in some aspects and for a certain constitution, and inversely, as we have just demonstrated.[37]

As for the third expression, which finishes (the ternary expressing) the primordial singularity (the Muhammedian wisdom), it is prayer (as-salâh), of which the prophet said: 'the freshness of my eyes is given to me in prayer' (that is to say that he finds in it his consolation);[38] for prayer is a contemplation and a secret call exchanged between God and His servant, conforming to the Divine Word: 'Remember me, I will remember you' (or: 'Name Me, I will name you': adhkurunî adhkhurkum).[39] According to the Divine Word faithfully transmitted since the Prophet, prayer is a cult the sense of which is shared between God and His servant, and so is related on the one hand to God and on the other to the individual: 'I have divided prayer between Me and My servant into two halves, one being due to Me, the other to My servant; and My servant will receive that for which he asks'. Thus (in the recitation of the surat al-fâtihah[40] which constitutes the principal text of the ritual prayer) the servant says; 'In the Name of God the Compassionate, (ar-rahmân) the Merciful (ar-rahîm)', and God replies: 'My servant mentions Me (or: remembers Me)'; the servant then says: 'Praise be to God, the Master of the Universes', and God says in His turn: 'My servant lends Me grace'; the servant continues: 'The Compassionate, the Merciful', and God

---

[37] The bad is 'good', not in so far as it is opposed to something good, but by its ontological foundation, which is necessarily positive, then, in its causality which necessarily implies positive factors, and finally, in its cosmic necessity.

[38] According to the Arabic metaphor, the eyes are refreshed when the bitterness and the burning of tears ceases.

[39] Koran II, 147.

[40] Koran I.

says: 'My servant lauds Me'; the servant recites: 'The King of the Day of Judgement', and God says: 'My servant glorifies Me, and submits himself to Me'. This is the first half of the prayer, that which relates to God – Exalted may He be! – exclusively. Next, the servant says: 'It is Thee whom we adore, and it is of Thee that we beg assistance'; and God says: 'This is shared between Me and My servant, and My servant will receive that which he asks'; this verse, then, expresses a mutual participation. When the servant then says: 'Lead us in the right way, the way of those to whom Thou hast been gracious, not of those against whom Thou art incensed, nor of those who have gone astray', God says: 'All that comes back to My servant, and My servant will receive that for which he asks'. The second half of the prayer then, is related exclusively to the individual, in the same way as the first half is related only to God. That makes one understand the (ritual) necessity of reciting this verse (in prayer); he who does not recite it does not accomplish the prayer shared between God and His servant.

Prayer is a secret call exchanged between God and the adorer; it is, then, also an invocation (*dhikr*), (this term meaning either: invocation, mentioned, call, remembrance). But, whoever invokes God, finds himself in the presence of God, according to the Divine Word (*hadîth qudsî*) faithfully transmitted since the Prophet: 'I witness the invocation of he who invokes Me' (*anâ jâlisu man dhakarani*); and he who finds himself in the presence of He whom he invokes, contemplates Him, if he is endowed with intellectual vision. That is the contemplation (*mushâhadah*) and the vision (*ru-yâ*); but he who does not have intellectual vision (*basar*) does not contemplate Him. It is by this actuality or absence of vision in the prayer that the adorer can judge of his own spiritual degree. If he does not see Him, let him then adore Him by faith 'as if he saw Him' (according to the definition that the Prophet gave in the *ihsân*, the spiritual virtue 'is to adore God as if thou didst see Him, and if thou dost not see Him, He however sees thee'); let him imagine Him in front of him (literally: in his *qiblah*, ritual orientation) when he addresses his prayer to Him,[41] and let him 'lend his hearing' to that which God will reply to him. If he is the

---

[41] According to the Word of the Prophet: 'In truth God is present in the *qiblah* of every one of you'; the commentator an-Nâbulusî adds: 'This imaginative concentration is not contrary to the faith when one exercises it consciously knowing that one is powerless to understand God by imagination; for it is said in the Koran: We will impose on each soul only the obligation of which it is capable'. (Koran II, 286, VI, 153, VII, 40.)

imam (that is to say he who guides the prayer in common) of his own microcosm and the angels who pray with him – and each one who accomplishes this prayer is *imam*, without doubt, since the angels pray behind the adorer who prays alone, as the Prophetic Word attests, – he realizes by that the function of the Divine Messenger in the prayer, in the sense that he is the representative of God; when he recites (in straightening up from bowing): 'God hears he who lauds Him'; he announces to himself and those who pray behind him that God has heard him, and the angels and the others present reply: 'Our Lord, Praise to Thee!' For it is God who says through the mouth of His adorer: 'God hears those who praise Him' (this enunciation, like the response, being rule in the ritual prayer). Look then to what sublime function the prayer corresponds and to what end it leads. He who does not reach the degree of spiritual vision (*ar-rû'yâh*) in prayer has not fully realized and does not yet find there 'the freshness of the eyes'; for he does not see He to whom he addressed himself. If he does not hear that which God answers him in the prayer, he is not one of those who 'lends his hearing': he who is not present in front of his Lord when he prays, and does not hear Him and does not see Him, is not consciously in a state of prayer, and the Koranic Word 'who lends his hearing and is witness' does not apply to him. That which distinguishes prayer from all other rite (of common obligation), is that it excludes, for as long as it lasts, every other occupation (ritual or profane); but that which is the greatest in everything that it involves in words and gestures, is the mention of God (or the invocation of God: *dhikr-ullâh*). Moreover we have already explained in the *Futûhât* the state of perfectly virile man at the time of prayer. For God says (in the Koran): 'Prayer prevents transgressions of passion and the grave sin',[42] precisely, because the adorer is beholden to occupy himself with nothing but the prayer, as long as it lasts; 'but certainly, the invocation of God (*dhikr-ullâh*) is greater . . .'.[43] That which, applied to prayer, must be understood in the sense that the invocation (or call) addressed by God to His servant, at the time of the Divine reply to the request and the praise, is greater than that which the adorer addresses to God; for the grandeur is attributable to God alone – Exalted may He be! It is why He says: 'God knows that which you do'[44] and He says: '. . .

---

[42] Koran XXIX, 44.
[43] Ibid.
[44] Ibid.

whoever listens or whoever is witness . . .'[45] that is to say, who listens to the call (*dhikr*) that God addresses him in the prayer.

In this order of ideas we will also say : from the fact that existence flows by an intelligible movement from that very thing which produced the world from its state of non-manifestation to its manifestation, the ritual prayer synthesizes all the movements, which are (essentially) three, that is to say : an ascending movement, which corresponds to the upright position of the adorer, a horizontal movement, analogous to the inclined position, and a descending movement, indicated by the ritual prostration. The ascending movement corresponds moreover to the attitude 'par excellence' of man, whereas the tendence of the animal is horizontal, and the tendence of the plants is descending (their nutritive organs being the roots). As for the minerals, they have no movement of their own : when a stone is moved it is obeying an out-side impulsion.'[46]

Concerning the Word of the Prophet : 'The freshness of my eyes is given to me in prayer' its form expressly indicates that the state in question is not the result of an individual tendence, since the revelation (*tajallī*) of God in prayer is a Divine act and not an act of he who prays. If the Prophet had not mentioned this state of things concerning him, that would imply that he had received the order to accomplish the prayer without God revealing Himself to him. But since this order was the expression of a Divine favour towards him, the Prophet said : 'The freshness of my eyes has been given to me in prayer'. Now, this 'freshness of the eyes' is none other than the contemplation of the Well-beloved, contemplation which (according to the meanings of 'repose' and 'immobility' implied in the term *qurrah*, 'freshness') re-poses the eye of the lover and makes him immobile in his vision, so that he sees no other things at the same time, voluntarily or involun-tarily. It is for that reason that it is forbidden to turn round (from the

[45] In this there is really a warning for he who has a heart, or who listens and is witness (or: is conscious) (Koran XL, 36).

[46] According to the commentator al-Qashânî the three 'existential' move-ments which retrace the gestures of the faithful and the natural tendencies of the three categories of organic beings, are principially: the movement of the Creator descending, who withdraws so to speak from the Principle to establish the foundations of the universe, then the upward movement of the Creator, which brings to bloom the degrees of manifestation starting from their material base, and finally the movement of 'horizontal' expansion of the manifestation to its diverse levels of actuality. This corresponds strictly to the three universal tendences which Hindus call 'gunas'.

ritual orientation) during prayer, for all turning aside is a theft of Satan from the adoration, by which he prevents the adorer from contemplating his Well-beloved. If it was really his Well-beloved, (that he tries to contemplate), this adorer who turns aside his face from his ritual orientation, would certainly not turn aside; but every man is conscious of his own state of soul, and he knows well what is his spiritual attitude during the adoration, for : 'Man is witness of himself, whatever the excuse he proffers';[47] that is to say he can quite well distinguish the falsehood of the sincerity in his soul, since it is impossible that a being is ignorant of his own state, object of his direct consent (*dhawq*).

That which one specifies by the term 'prayer' (*salâh*) involves again other distinctions; for according to the Koranic text, God orders us on one hand to address to Him the prayer, and, on the other, He tells us that He dispenses us Mercy from His own 'prayer' (*salâh*) that He 'prays' over us,[48] so that prayer goes from us towards him, and from Him to us. When it is He who 'prays', He does it by virtue of His Name the Last (*al-âkhir*), for in this respect His manifestation supposes the previous manifestation of the created being. But, this (this Divine revelation according to the sense of the Name the Last) is none other than the determination of God that the adorer 'creates' in his ritual orientation, be it by his intellectual vision, be it by his dogmatic belief. It is the conformation of the Divinity to the belief : the Divinity varies according to the capacity of its 'place' (or receptacle) of revelation; thus Junayd expressed it when he replied to the question (on the connection which exists between the knowledge of God and he who knows) : 'The colour of water is the colour of its receptacle'; this is certainly a masterly reply, touching the nature of that which is in question; that is, (meaning : the Divine determination 'created' at the time of the prayer) – God, in so far as He 'prays' over us. On the other hand if it is we who pray, it is to us that the Name the Last is implied, in the sense that we are then implicated in this Name, because of that which we explained just now on the Divine condition corresponding to this Name;[49] we are then close to Him, in the measure of our own (spiritual) state, so that He looks at us only by virtue of the

[47] Koran LXXV, 14–15.

[48] That is to say he blesses us, the word *salâh* having the double meaning to 'pray' and 'to bless'.

[49] That is to say : we come 'after', since our prayer presupposes someone to whom it is addressed, meaning God.

(spiritual) form that we ourselves manifest; for it is certainly he who prays who always stays behind.[50] It is said in the Koran: ('Dost thou not see that all exalt God, those who are in the heavens and on the earth, and the birds that fly in rows?). Each one knows his prayer and his worship';[51] that is to say he knows his own degree of 'tardiness' (or inferiority) in the adoration (in relation to that which would be a completely adequate adoration) of his Lord, and (he knows) his praise which (conforms to) whatever his (spiritual) capacity (al-isti'dâd) can confirm of the Divine transcendence. 'Is there anything which does not exalt His praise?'[52] that is to say the praise of his Lord, the Wise, He who forgives; ('but you do not understand their praise'): we would not know how to understand their praise (the ways of praise) of the whole universe distinctly, each thing taken separately.

According to a certain point of view, the pronoun, in the sentence: 'Is there anything which does not exalt His praise?' refers to the thing itself, that is to say that the creature praises by that which it is. This is analogous to that which we were saying of the believer, meaning that he praises the Divinity which conforms to his own belief and connects himself to it in this way; but, all acts return to their author, so that the believer praises himself, as the work praises its artist, all perfection and all lack that it manifests falling back on its author. In the same way, the Divinity (as such, which) conforms to the belief is created by he who concentrates on It, and It is his own work. In praising that which he believes, the believer praises his own soul, it is because of that that he condemns other beliefs than his own; if he was just, he would not do it; only, he who is fixed on a certain particular adoration, is necessarily ignorant (of the intrinsic truths of other beliefs), in the same way that his belief in God implies a negation of the other forms of belief. If he understood the sense of the word of Junayd: 'The colour of water is the colour of its receptacle', he would admit the validity of all beliefs, and he would recognise God in every form and every object of faith. The fact is that he has not the knowledge (of God) but relies uniquely on the opinion (zann) of which the Divine Word speaks: 'I conform Myself to the opinion that My servant has of Me', which means: 'I manifest Myself to My adorer

---

[50] That is to say: who limits or who restrains, who determines the contents as function of the receptacle.

[51] Koran XXIV, 41.

[52] Koran XVII, 46.

only in the form of his belief; so, let him generalize, if he wishes, or let him determine'. The Divinity conforming to the belief is that which can be defined, and it is That, the God, which the heart can contain (according to the Divine Word : 'Neither My heavens nor My earth can contain Me, but the heart of My faithful servant contains Me'). For the Absolute Divinity cannot be contained in anything since It is the very Essence of things and Its own Essence : one does not say of some being that he contains himself; on the other hand, nor does one say that he does not contain himself. Understand then! God – May He be Exalted! – speaks the truth, and it is He who guides on the right way.

Glossary of Terms

al-'abd : the servant; the slave : indicates in religious language the adorer, and more generally the creature in so much as he depends on his Lord (*rabb*) pp. 81, 124.

'Abd al-Karîm al-Jîlî, ibn Ibrâhîm : ca. 1365 - ca. 1417; Sufi. He wrote amongst others the celebrated book of *Al-Insân al-Kâmil* : 'Universal Man', pp. 4, 43.

'Abd ar-Razzâq al-Qashânî : Sufi of the 13th century, commentator on Ibn 'Arabî, p. 6.

Abu Saîd al-Kharrâz : celebrated Sufi from Baghdad, died in Cairo in 899, p. 36.

adab : education, politeness, tact, p. 32.

'adam : see *'udum.*

adhkurunî adhkurkum : 'Remember me and I will remember you' or : 'Name me and I will name thee' Koran II. 147 cf., p. 127.

al-'adl : Justice, Equality; Divine Name, p. 28.

afâda : overflow, emanate; see *fayd.*

al-af'al plural of *al-fi'l* : action, activity; *al-af'âl al-ilâhiyah* : the Divine Activities, p. 98.

ahad : one; see : *ahadiyah,* pp. 64, 66.

ahâdith : plural of *hadîth.*

al-ahadiyah : the unity; in Sufism : the Supreme Unity which makes the object of no distinctive knowledge, which is not therefore accessible to the creature as such; it is only God Himself who knows Himself in His Unity. As a spiritual state, Unity requires the extinction of all trace of the created, pp. 56, 57.

ahadiyat al-kuthrah : the unity of the multiple, p. 66.

ahl al-haqâïq : 'the family of Essential Realities' : men who contemplate the Essential Realities : see *haqîqah,* p. 32.

'Aissa : Jesus, p. 68.

al-âkhir : the Last; Divine Name, pp. 16, 84, 131.

'alem al-amthâl : synonymous to *'alem al-mithâl.*

'alem al-jabarût : 'The world of the All Powerful' sometimes identified to *'alem al-arwâh* : 'the world of the (pure) spirits'; the informal manifestation; see also *hâhût*.

'alem al-khayâl : the world of imagination; see *'alem al-mithal*, p. 59.

'alem al-mithâl or *'alem al-amthâl* : 'the world of analogies', the formal world, as much psychic as corporal; it corresponds to *'âlam al-khayâl* : 'the world of imagination', p. 30.

al-'alî : the Pupil; Divine Name, p. 35.

al-alîn : the superior (spirits) : the angels closest to God, p. 76.

al-amr : the order, the command; in theology : the Divine Command symbolized by the word of creation *kun*, 'Be' : 'His Command, *(amruhu)* when He willeth a thing, is only that He saith unto it, Be; and it is' (Koran XXXVI, 81). The Command corresponds then, to the Word, the word *amr* having moreover the latter sense in Aramaïc. The two following passages from the Koran affirm implicitly the identity of the Command and of the Divine Word *(kalimah)* or Verb. 'Verily the likeness of Jesus in the eyes of God is as the likeness of Adam : God created him out of dust, and then said unto him, Be; and he was' (III. 54) 'The Messiah Jesus the Son of Mary is the apostle of God, and His Word, *(kalimatuhu)* which he conveyed into Mary, and a spirit proceeding from him' (IV, 170). On the relation Word-Spirit see under *rûh*. Al-*amr* often takes the sense of 'reality', 'act', 'actual thing'; the Divine Command corresponds to the Pure Act and is opposed as such to the pure passivity of Nature *(at-tabî'ah)* : The plural of *amr*, *umûr*, signifies 'realities', for example in the Koranic expression : 'To Him will the realities *(umûr)* return'. It is a question, obviously, of the essential realities of things, which will return to God; but, these correspond to the multiple 'aspects' of the Command or the Divine Word, pp. 8, 10, 12, 27, 31, 40, 44, 59, 74, 79, 93, 104, 116, 121, 126.

anâ jâlisu man dhakaranî : 'I am the Companion of he who invokes Me' *(hadîth qudsî)*, p. 128.

anfâs : plural of *nafas*.

al-'aqil : the one who knows, the intelligent one. The ternary : *al-maqil* (the one who knows), *al-ma'qûl* (the known) *al-'aql* (the intellect, the knowledge) plays an important part in metaphysics, p. 116.

al-'aql : the intellect; *al-'aql al-awwal* : the First Intellect, analogous to Supreme Pen *(al-kalam)* and to *ar-rûh*; it corresponds to Plotinian *Noûs*, p. 111.

al-'arsh : the (Divine) Throne, p. 125.

al-arsh al-muhît : the (Divine) Throne that englobes all things, p. 125.

'assâ : staff; past definite of 'to disobey', p. 112.

Assaf ibn Barkhiyâ : the name of a wise man, companion of Solomon, p. 88.

asmâ plural of *ism* : name; *al-asmâ al ilâhiyah*, are Divine Names which are subdivided into *asmâ dhâtiyah*, 'Essential Names' this is to say Names which express the pure transcendence of the Essence, and *asmâ sî-fâtiyah*, 'Qualitative Names', which express the Universal Qualities; the latter comprise equally the *asmâ af 'aliyah*, the Names expressing the Divine Activities.

asmâ al-husna : 'the Most Beautiful Names' or 'The Names of Beauty'; Koranic expression which denotes the Divine Names, p. 8.

al-awwaliyah : the primordiality, p. 16.

al-awwal : the First, Divine Name, pp. 16, 84.

al-'ayân; plural of *'ayn* : the first essences or determinations of things; *al-a'yân ath-thâbitah* : the 'unchanging essences' or principial possibilities, the archetypes.

al-'ayn : the Essence, the First Determination, the eye, the source; *al-'ayn ath-thâbitah* sometimes also simply *al-'ayn* : the unchanging Essence, the Archetype, the fundamental possibility of a being or of a thing, pp. 8, 9, 22, 30, 35, 37, 43, 52, 62, 64, 65, 67, 89, 113, 122.

'aynah : its (or his) essence (acc.) : possessive form of *'ayn*.

'aynuh : its (or his) essence (nom.); possessive form of *'ayn*.

al-azal : the Eternity without beginning; see also *al-qidam*, p. 16.

al-'azîz : the Powerful, the Precious, the Dear; Divine Name, p. 81.

barakah : benediction, spiritual influence.

al-bâri : the Producer (aspect of Creator); Divine Name, p. 94.

al-barzakh : the Isthmus; as figurative; the intermediary between the two degrees of existence, p. 11.

basar : sight, intellectual sight, p. 128.

al-bashar : man; man made of flesh, p. 76.

bâtin : Interior, Hidden; contrary to *zâhir* : Exterior, Apparent. One distinguishes the 'interior science' (*al-'ilm al-bâtin*), meaning esoteric, Sufi science, from the 'exterior science' (*al-'ilm az-zâhir*) the doctors of the Law. *Al-bâtin*, 'the Interior', is one of the Koranic Names of God, pp. 16, 33, 84, 110.

Bilqîs : Arabic name of the Queen of Sheba, p. 83.

as-salâh : the (ritual) prayer, pp. 127, 131.

as-sîfât : the qualities or attributes; *as-sîfât al-ilâhiyah* : the Divine Qualities or Attributes. See also *dhât*, p. 98.

as-sirat al-mustaqîm : the Right Way, p. 92.

as-surah : the form *as-surat al-ilâhiyah* : the Divine Form, pp. 11, 18.

adh-dhât : the Essence, the Quiddity. The *dhât* of a being is the subject to which are referred all its qualities (*sifât*); the qualities differ between themselves but not in their attachment to the same subject, pp. 8, 65, 75, 98, 123.

dhâtiyah : essential (a); see also *adh-dhât*, p. 13.

adh-dhawq : the savour; figurative : the intuition, pp. 20, 131.

dhikr : souvenir, mention; as a rite : invocation, pp. 128, 130.

dhikr-ullâh : invocation of God, souvenir of God, mention of God, p. 129.

al-fass : the setting (of a gem), p. 1, 2.

al-faqir ilâ-llâh : 'the poor in comparison to God' according to the Koranic expression : 'O men, you are poor (*fuqarâ*) in relation to God, and God is the Rich, the Glorious; (XXXV. 16) in particular, every man following a contemplative path is called *faqîr ilâ-llâh* or simply *faqîr*; the Persian equivalent is 'dervish' (*darwish*). The application of the name 'fakir' to ascertain ascetics of low category exhibiting themselves in public places in India, originates from a corruption of the original sense of the word, p. 107.

al-faqr : indigence, poverty : spiritual poverty, p. 66.

al-fard : the singular, p. 116.

al-fâtihah : 'That which opens' the first verse of the Koran, ritual prayer of Islam, p. 127.

al-fayd : the overflowing, the flow, or flux, the effusion, the emanation; in metaphysics, this should not be conceived as a substantial emanation : the 'overflowing' of the Infinite Being on the relative possibilities is obviously not a 'sortie' of the One outside Himself, p. 9.

al-fayd al-aqdas : 'The Most Saintly Effusion', the principial manifestation, supraformal, pp. 9, 10.

al-fayd al muqaddas : 'the Saintly Effusion', the manifestation of God in forms, p. 10.

al-fitrâh : primordial nature, uncorrupted, p. 94.

fusûs : settings (of gems); the plural of (*fass*).

al-fuqarâ : the indigents, the poor; the poor in spirit, p. 67.

al-furqân : discrimination; Koranic name of the Book of Revelation – or of revelation in general – under its aspect of law. See also *al-qur'an*, pp. 12, 54.

al-ghaffâr : the Forgiving; Divine Name, p. 28.

ghanî binafsihi : litt : rich by oneself, that is to say : independent, p. 9.

al-ghayb : the mysterious, the non-manifested, p. 30.

al-ghayb al-mutlaq : the Absolute Mystery, the pure non-manifestation, p. 30.

al-Ghazzâlî, Abû Hâmid Muhammed : 1058-1111, great theologian and the reviver of the religious sciences of Islam, p. 41.

al-habâ : the universal plastic substance, the 'materia prima'.

al-hadarât : the (Divine) Presences, or the modalities of the Divine Presence in contemplation. One distinguishes the principal 'Presences' as follows :

  1. *hadarât al-ghayb al-mutlaq* : the (Divine) Presence in the Absolute non-manifestation.
  2. *hadarât al-ghayb-al-mudâfî* : the (Divine) Presence in the relative non-manifestation.
  3. *hadarât ash-shahâdat al-mutlaqah* : the (Divine) Presence in the absolute manifestation.
  4. *al-hadarât al-jam'iyah* : the integral (Divine) Presence, p. 30.

[138]

hadarât al-khayâl : the (Divine) Presence in the world of imagination : see also : *'alem al-mithâl*, p. 47.

hadîth : sentence, Word of the Prophet transmitted outside the Koran by a chain of known intermediaries; there are two sorts of *ahâdith* : *hadîth qudsî* (sacred sentence) denotes a direct revelation, where God speaks in the first person through the mouth of the Prophet; *hadîth nabawî* (prophetic sentence) denotes a direct revelation, where the Prophet speaks through his own person, pp. 18, 40, 125, 128.

al-hâhût : the Essential Nature of God; derived from the Divine Name *huwa* 'He', and formed by analogy with the following terms, which we cite according to their hierarchical descendancy.

> *al-lahut* : the Divine Nature (Creator).
> *al-jabarût* : the Power, the Divine Immensity, the informal world.
> *al-malakût* : the angelic reign, the spiritual world.
> *an-nâsût* : human nature, especially the corporal form of man, pp. 69, 97.

al-hakam : the Judge; Divine Name, p. 28.

al-hakîm : the Wise; Divine Name, pp. 28, 81.

al-hâl plural : *ahwâl* : the state, spiritual state; one sometimes opposes *hâl* (state) to *maqâm* (spiritual station) : in this case, the former is considered as transient, the latter as stable, p. 22.

al-hamîd : the Glorious, Praiseworthy; Divine Name, p. 27.

al-haqâïq : plural of *haqîqah,* pp. 6, 14, 86, 98.

al-haqîqah : the truth, the reality : in Sufism : the Divine Truth of Reality, the Essential Reality of things. The Word of the Prophet : *'likulli dhî haqqin haqîqah'*, 'to all real things there corresponds a Divine Reality (or Truth)', pp. 28, 36, 73, 110, 117.

haqîqat al-haqâïq : 'The Truth of Truths' or 'Reality of Realities', analogous to Logos; it is considered as the intangible 'Isthmus', *(barzakh)* intermediary between the Divine Being and the cosmos, p. 11.

al-haqq : the Truth or the Reality; in Sufism, *al-haqq* denotes the Divinity in so much as it is distinguished from the creature, *(al-khalq)*. See also : *haqîqah*, pp. 8, 10, 11, 33, 40, 44, 53.

al-harf : singular of *hurûf*, p. 115.

al-haybah : the reverential awe, the fear of the Divine Majesty, p. 16.

al-hayrah : consternation, perplexity, pp. 3, 38, 99.

al-hikam : plural of *hikmah,* wisdom.

al-hikmah : wisdom, pp. 1, 96.

al-hikmat al-'aliyah : the elevated Wisdom : . . . *al-fardiyah* : the Wisdom of the singularity; . . . *al-haqqiyah* : the Wisdom of (Divine) Truth; . . . *al-ilâhiyah* : the Divine Wisdom; . . . *al-muhaymiyah* : the Wisdom of (unbounded) Love; . . . *an-nafathiyah* : the Wisdom of the Divine Inspiration; . . . *an-nubûwiyah* : the Wisdom of Prophecy; . . . *an-nûriyah* : the Luminous Wisdom; . . . *al-quddûsiyah* : the Holy Wisdom, the Wisdom of Holiness; . . . *-ar-rahmâniyah* : the Merciful Wisdom, the Wisdom of the (Divine) Mercy; . . . *as-subûhiyah* : the Wisdom of the

[139]

Transcendence, the Wisdom of the Exaltation (of God); . . . *al-ulûhiyah* : the Sublime Wisdom, the Wisdom of the Divine Sublimity, pp. 8, 20, 32, 35, 40, 46, 56, 59, 68, 83, 96, 116.

al-himmah : the spiritual will, the force of decision, aspiration towards God, pp. 52, 93, 121.

al-hudûr : the presence, state of spiritual concentration, p. 21.

al-hudûth : ephemerity; opposite to *al-qidam* (eternity), p. 105.

al-hukm : the principle, the judgement, pp. 15, 91, 109.

hulûl : localisation, localised immanence of God; heterodoxy, p. 72.

al-hurûf : the letters of the alphabet and following, the sounds they represent.

huwa : 'He', Divine Name.

al-huwiyah; derived from the pronoun *huwa*, 'He' : the Ipseity, the Divine Aseity, the Supreme 'Self', pp. 33, 72, 78, 86.

Idris : Enoch, p. 35.

'ifrit : Afrit, sort of genie, pp. 85, 88.

al-ihsân : spiritual virtue, interior beauty. According to the Prophet, it consists in that 'thou dost adore God as if thou saw Him; if thou dost not see Him, however, He sees thee' (*hadîth Jibrâîl*). We note this fundamental ternary, commented by the Prophet : *al-islâm*, the abandon to the Divine Will, *al-iman*, the faith and *al-ihsân*, the sanctifying virtue, pp. 47, 128.

al-ikhlâs : purity, sincerity, p. 66.

ilâh : Divinity, p. 41.

al-'ilm : the knowledge, science, p. 91.

imâm : model, prototype : ritually : he who presides over the common prayer; chief of religious community, p. 129.

insân : man, p. 12.

al-insân al-kabir : 'The Great Man', the macrocosm, according to the adage : 'the cosmos is a great man, and man is a small cosmos', p. 11.

al-insân al-kâmil : 'Perfect Man' or 'Universal Man'; Sufi term for he was has realized all the degrees of Being; denotes also the permanent prototype of man, p. 12, 30, 98.

al-islâm : submission, abandon to the Divine Will; see under : *al-ihsân*, p. 92.

al-isti'dâd : predisposition, aptitude, preparation to receive, virtuality, pp. 9, 21, 57, 132.

al-jabarût : the world of the All Powerful, or the Divine Immensity; see also *hâhût*, p. 30.

al-jabbâr : the All Powerful : Divine Name, p. 28.

al-jam'îyat al-ilâhiyah : the Divine synthesis, p. 11.

al-janâb al-ilâhî : the Divine side, p. 11.

al-jannah : paradise, p. 58.

al-jasad : the concrete or subtle body, p. 51.

al-jawhar al-hayûlâni the first substance, the 'materia prima' litt : the 'substantial jewel', p. 123.

al-jinn – the genii, beings belonging to the psychic world, p. 88.

al-Junayd, Abu-l-Qâsim died in 910, celebrated master of Sufism, named the 'Head of the Band', p. 131.

al-kalimah : the Word, the Verb, p. 2.

al-kamâl : the perfection, plenitude, infinity, pp. 38, 99, 105.

kashf : intuition, litt : the withdrawing of a veil or curtain, pp. 47, 111.

al-kashf al-ilâhî : Divine Intuition, the knowledge of the Essential possibilities of God, pp. 11, 23.

katab-Allâhu 'alâ nafsihi-r-rahmah : 'He hath prescribed unto Himself, Mercy' (Koran VI, 12), p. 84.

kathîf : gross, concrete, corporal, p. 17.

al-kawn : the cosmos, the universe, pp. 8, 59.

al-khass : the particular one, man of the elite, p. 107.

khalaqa : create; see also *khalq*.

al-khalîfah : the representative, pp. 12, 109.

al-khalîl; the intimate friend; *khalîl-Allâh* : the Friend of God, surname of Abraham, p. 40.

al-khatam : the seal, see also *khâtim*, p. 1.

khâtim or *khatam* : seal; *khâtim al wilâyâ* 'the Seal of Saintliness'; *khâtim an-nubuwwâ* : 'the Seal of the Prophets'; the former expression often refers to Christ at the time of his second coming, the latter always to Muhammed, p. 116.

khâtim-al-awliyâ : 'the Seal of the Saints' synonymous to *khâtim al-wilâyâ*, p. 25.

khâtim ar-rusul : the 'Seal of the (Divine) Messengers', p. 25.

al-khayâl : the faculty of imagination; it is purely passive, be it with regard to the faculty of conjecture (*al-wahm*), which confers on it the character of illusion, be it with regard to the Intellect (*al-'aql*) or of the Spirit (*ar-rûh*) which can imprint on it prophetic visions, pp. 48, 52.

Al-Khidr : name of a mysterious person whom Moses met near to the fountain of life, p. 104.

al-kufr : the unbelieving, p. 72.

kun : Be ! the 'fiat', Creator's Order; see also *al-amr*, pp. 8, 73.

ladunnî : 'close to me'; adjective which serves to denote immediate Divine inspiration, p. 103.

al-lâhût : the Divine Nature (Creator) : see *al-hâhût*, p. 69.

lam yakun thumma kâna : 'he was not, and then he was', p. 89.

latîf; fine, subtle, non-apparent, p. 17.

al-lawh al-mahfûz : the Guarded Table.

mâ : see : *mâhiyah*, p. 109.

mahal : place, station, halt, abode, p. 38.

mâhiyah : word derived from relative and interrogative pronoun *mâ*, 'that', 'what', and signifying the quiddity of a thing, p. 109.

majlâ : place of irradiation, of revelation, plane of reflection of Divine *tajallî*, 'theatre', pp. 38, 100.

al-makân : the place, p. 51.

al-malâ' al-a'lâ : the Supreme Assembly, the Archangels and the Beings closest to God, p. 75.

al-malaïkat al-muhaymiyah : 'The angels lost in love'; the Supreme Angels absorbed in the Divine Being.

al-malakût : the permanent Sovereignty, the celestial and angelic reign; of the Koranic verse : 'It is He who holds in His Hand the Sovereignty of all things' XXXV. 83; see also *hâhût*, p. 89.

man'arafa nafsahu'arafa rabbah : 'He who knows himself, knows his Lord' (*hadîth*), p. 117.

maqamât : stations; plural of *maqam*, p. 45.

al-mar'âh : the woman, p. 121.

mathal; analogous, similar : see *'alem al-mithâl*, p. 89.

al-mawjûdât al'ayniyah : the individual existences; see *wujûd 'ayni*, p. 14.

minhâj : way, rule, p. 101.

mishkât : niche, tabernacle; the verse of the 'Light'; 'God is the Light of heaven and earth : the symbol of His Light is like a tabernacle (*mishkât*) in a wall; in the tabernacle there is a lamp; the lamp is within glass; the glass appears as it were a shining star . . . XXIV. 35, p. 25.

al-mubâshara : the tenderness, the action of making somebody happy, p. 76.

muhyi-d-dîn : reviver of religion, p. 1.

al-mumkinât, plural of *mumkin* : the possibilities; one distinguishes logically between *mumkin* (possible), *wâjib* (necessary) and *jâïz* (contingent); from the metaphysical point of view, the possible is brought back fundamentally to the necessary, since all possibility has necessarily the reality that it contains by its nature, p. 62.

Mûsâ : Arabic name of Moses, p. 100.

musawwî : right, equal, homogenous, p. 9.

mushâhadah : contemplation : see also *shahâdah*, p. 128.

mutawahham : illusory, imaginary; word derived from the same root as *wahm*, p. 64.

nabî : prophet; see also *rasûl*, pp. 25, 26, 27.

nafas ar-rahmân : the 'Breath of Mercy', called also *an-nafas ar-rahmâni* : the Merciful Breath; the Divine Mercy considered as manifesting principle, and thence as almost maternal power of God. See also *rahmah*, pp. 75, 76, 89, 105, 118, 122.

naffasa : blow, breath, dilate, console; see also *nafas,* pp. 76, 89, 105, 124.

an-nafs : the soul, the psyche, that is to say the subtle reality of the individual : the 'I'. In its opposition to the spirit (*rûh*) or the intellect (*'aql*), the *nafs* appears in a negative aspect, because of being constituted by the totality of individual and egocentric tendencies. One may distinguish, however, between :

    1. *an-nafs al-haywâniyah* : the 'animal' soul, that is to say the soul in so much as it obeys passively natural impulses.

2. *an-nafs al-ammârah* : 'the soul which commands', that is to say the passionate and egoistic soul.

3. *an-nafs al-lawwâmah* : 'the soul that blames', that is to say the soul conscious of its imperfections.

4. *an-nafs al-mutmaïnnah* : 'the soul at peace', that is to say the soul re-integrated in the Spirit, resting in the certitude. The three last expressions are Koranic, pp. 22, 77.

an-nafs al-kulliyah : the Universal Soul, which englobes all the individual souls; it corresponds to the Guarded Table (*al-lawh al-mahfûz*) and is opposed to the Spirit (*ar-rûh*) or First Intellect (*al-'aql al-awwal*); it is analogous to the psyche of Plotinus.

an-nafs al-wâhidah : the 'unique soul', from which were created all the individual souls; see *an-nafs al-kulliyah*, p. 18.

an-nâr : the fire, p. 119.

al-nâsût : the human nature; see *al-hâhût*, pp. 69, 97.

an-nisâ : woman, collective, p. 121.

nisab dhâtiyah : essential relations, relations inherent to the Divine Essence, p. 23.

an-nûr : the light; in metaphysics : the Divine Light, source of existence, pp. 9, 62, 63, 119.

nuzûl : litt : descent : the revelation in the particular sense of the term, p. 60.

Omar ibn al-Khattâb : name of a companion of the Prophet, who became the second Caliph.

al-qâbil : the receptacle, the substance which is passive and receptive, derived from the root QBL which signifies 'receive', 'place oneself in front of', pp. 9, 11, 22, 38.

al-qadr : the power, the predestination, the measure of the power inherent in a thing, p. 21.

al-qahhâr : the Subduer, the Victorious; Divine Name, p. 28.

al-qalb : the heart; supra-rational organ of intuition; which corresponds to the heart as thought corresponds to the brain. The fact that modern people localize in the heart, not intellectual intuition but sentiment, proves that with them it occupies the centre of the individuality.

al-qawâbil : plural of *qâbil*.

qiblah : ritual orientation, p. 128.

al-qidam : the eternity, the antiquity, p. 16.

al-qur'ân : the Koran, litt : 'the recitation' or 'the reading', in Sufi symbolism, this term considers the revelation under its aspect of immediate knowledge, non-differentiated. See also *al-furqân*, pp. 12, 54.

qurrah : repose, freshness, consolation, p. 130.

quwwatun malakûtiyah : 'a celestial force' or 'an angelic force', p. 89.

ar-râhah : repose, relaxation, p. 105.

ar-rabb : the Lord; Divine Name, p. 56.

ar-rahîm : He who is merciful (towards the beings); active form of the root RHM; see also *ar-rahmah*, pp. 83, 84, 85, 127.

ar-rahmah : the Mercy (Divine) : the same root RHM is to be found again in the two Divine Names : *ar-rahmân* (The Compassionate, He whose Mercy englobes everything) and *ar-rahîm* (The Merciful, He who saves by His Mercy) (Grace); the most simple word from the same root is *rahîm* : matrix, or the maternal aspect of the Divine Names, pp. 27, 84, 125.

ar-rahmân : the Compassionate; see *ar-rahmah*, pp. 28, 51, 83, 85, 118, 124, 127.

ar-rahmâniyah : the Divine integral Quality, corresponding to the Divine Name *ar-rahmân*; the Merciful Beatitude, pp. 53, 83, 119.

rasûl : apostle, messenger : in theology : Divine Apostle. It is in the role of messenger (*rasûl*) that a prophet (*nabî*) promulgates a new sacred law; all prophets are not necessarily *rasûl*, although enjoying Divine Inspiration, but all *rasûl* is implicitly *nabî*, pp. 25, 26, 27, 70.

ar-raqîb : the Observer : Divine Name, p. 80.

rawh : rest, joy, grace, justice, pp. 9, 74.

râyhan : myrrh; all perfumed plants, p. 74.

risâlah; the function of *rasûl*, of the messenger of God, pp. 97, 109.

ar-rubûbiyah : the Lordship; the Divine Quality corresponding to the Divine Name *ar-rabb*, the Lord, p. 56.

ar-rûh : the spirit, in Sufism, this word has the following principal significances :

1. The Divine Spirit, so, uncreated (*ar-rûh al-ilâhî*), also called *ar-rûh al-quds*, the Holy Spirit.
2. The Universal Spirit, created, (*ar-rûh al-kullî*).
3. The individual spirit or more exactly polarized with regard to an individual.
4. The vital spirit, intermediary between the soul and the body. Koran : 'They will ask thee concerning the spirit; tell them; the spirit was created at the command (*amr*) of my Lord' (XCII 84). Christ is called *Rûh Allâh*, 'Spirit of God'. See also *amr*, pp. 68, 96, 98.

ar-rûh-al-âmîn : 'the faithful Spirit', name of the Archangel Gabriel, p. 69.

ar-rûh al-manâwi : the intellectual spirit, p. 69.

rusul : plural of *rasûl*.

ru'-yâ : sight, vision, action of perceiving, pp. 8, 128.

rûyâ : vision; dream, p. 48.

Sahl at-Tûstarî, Abu Muhammed. 818-896, celebrated theologian and Sufi, from Tustar in Ahwâz; his 'Thousand sentences' have been collected by his disciples.

as-sa'îd : the blessed or fortunate, p. 56.

as-sakînah : the Divine Peace which dwells in a sanctuary or in the heart. The root SKN comprises the significances of 'immobility' (*sukûn*) and of 'habitation'. It is analogous to the Hebrew *shakhina*, the Divine Glory which dwells in the ark of alliance. From the Koranic verse : '. . . It is He who sendeth down *sakinah* into the hearts of the true believers, that they may increase in faith, beyond their former faith . . .' (XLVIII 4), p. 98.

as-Sâmiri : proper name from the Hebrew who induced the children of Israel to make the golden calf. Sometimes, this name is translated as 'the Samaritan', which is an anachronism only too evident, p. 68.

shahâdah; testimony, contemplation, objective perception, p. 120.

shahîd; witness; see also *shuhûd* and *shahâdah*, p. 80.

ash-sharâ'i : the diverse laws revealed; plural of *ash-sharî'ah*, p. 101.

sharî'ah : sacred law, revealed. Every Divine Messenger (*rasûl*) brings a new *sharî'ah* in conformity with the conditions of the cosmic and human cycle. *Sharî'ah* is opposed to *haqîqah*, Law sacred to Truth or Divine Realities the sacred Laws differ, whereas the Divine Reality is the same.

ash-shay' : the thing, pp. 8, 80.

sijjîn : prison; Koranic designation of inferior worlds, p. 68.

sijn : prison, p. 111.

sirr : secret, mystery. In Sufism, *as-sirr* denotes also the intimate and ineffable centre of the consciousness, the 'point of contact' between the individual and his Divine principle, p. 8.

as-sitr : the veil, the cover, p. 72.

as-suryân : the process(es), the propagation, p. 122.

at-tabî'ah : The Nature; *Tabî'at al-kull* : the Universal Nature. It is an aspect of the passive 'plastic' source, of the Universal Substance (*al-habâ*) : it is this substance in so far as generator of the world, from whence its maternal nature. Ibn 'Arabi attributes it to a co-extensive reality of all the universal manifestation and identifies it to 'the Breath of Mercy', pp. 11, 37, 72, 75.

at-tâbût : the ark (in which Moses was exposed in the Nile), p. 97.

at-tajallî : the unveiling, the revelation, the irradiation, pp. 8, 9, 57, 60, 89.

tajalliyât : plural of *tajallî*.

takwîn : 'existentiation', creation, p. 124.

tanfîs : relief, p. 77.

at-tanzîh : withdrawal, exaltation, affirmation of the Divine transcendence; contrary : *tashbih* : comparison, similitude affirmation of symbolism. The two affirmations are to be found united in the Koranic words as follows : 'Nothing is equal to Him' (= *tanzîh*), and 'it is He who hears and who sees (= *tashbîh*)', pp. 32, 37, 64.

tasbîh : praise; the action of attributing to God all perfection, p. 13.

at-tashbîh : the resemblance, the analogy, the symbolism; see *at-tanzîh*, pp. 32, 37, 64.

taqdîs : sanctification; action of proclaiming God 'Saintly', that is to say exempt from all imperfection or limit, p. 13.

tayibah : good, sweet smelling, p. 125.

thalathatun : fem : *thalathun* : three, p. 123.

al-'ubûdiyah : the quality of servant, perfect adorer, p. 51.

al-'udum, sometimes also called *'adam* : the non-existence : the absence, the non-being, nothingness. In Sufism, this expression comprises on the one hand a positive sense, that of non-manifestation, the fundamental state being situated beyond the existence or even beyond the One, and on the other hand a negative sense, that of privation, of relative nothingness, pp. 23, 35, 89.

al-ulûhiyah : word derived from *ilâh,* 'Divinity', and signifying the 'Quality of God' or 'Quality of Divinity', not in the sense of a particular Divine Quality but as total Divine Nature, pp. 34, 72.

al-umûr : plural of *al-amr;* the (Divine) Commandments.

al-umûr al-kulliyah : the Universal Realities, the 'Universal Ones', p. 13.

umûrun 'adamiyah : non-existent realities, that is to say non-manifested, p. 36.

al-uns : the confiding intimacy : opposed to *al-haybah,* p. 16.

al-wahhâb; the Giver : Divine Name, p. 28.

al-wahî : the (Divine) Inspiration, p. 59.

wâhid; unique, only; see *wâhidiyah,* p. 64.

al-wâhidiyah : (Divine) Uniqueness; it is distinguished from the Divine Unity (*ahadiyah*) which is beyond all distinctive knowledge, whereas 'Uniqueness' appears in the differentiated, just as fundamental distinctions appear in it.

al-wahm : the faculty of conjecture, opinion; see also *al-khayâl,* pp. 48, 52, 64, 70.

al-wâlî : the Lord : Divine Name, p. 28.

al-walî : the Saint; man of God, pp. 25, 27.

al-wârith : the Inheritor; Divine Name, p. 27.

al-wâsi' : the Vast; Divine Name, p. 28.

al-wilâyâ : the saintliness, p. 25.

al-wujûd : the One, the Existence, pp. 8, 23, 35, 44, 62, 105, 111.

wujûd 'aynî : determined existence, individual, gifted with substance, p. 14.

al-wujuh : the faces, the aspects; plural of *wajh.*

al-yaqîn : the certitude, p. 111.

zâhir; exterior, apparent; contrary to *bâtin;* see under this word. *az-zâhir,* 'the Exterior' or 'the Apparent', is one of the Koranic names of God, pp. 16, 33, 110.

az-zann : the thought, the opinion, p. 132.